AS RAIN
THAT FALLS

BOOKS BY CHARLES E. MILLER, C.M.

To Sow the Seed*
A Sense of Celebration
Communicating Christ**
Repentance and Renewal***
Announcing the Good News**
Breaking the Bread**
Until He Comes***
Living in Christ
Making Holy the Day
Love in the Language of Penance
Opening the Treasures
The Word Made Flesh**

*with Oscar J. Miller, C.M.
**with Oscar J. Miller, C.M. and Michael M. Roebert
***with John A. Grindel, C.M.

AS RAIN
THAT FALLS

Homiletic Reflections
for the
Weekdays of Advent and Lent

CHARLES E. MILLER, C.M.

ALBA · HOUSE   NEW · YORK

SOCIETY OF ST. PAUL, 2187 VICTORY BLVD., STATEN ISLAND, NEW YORK 10314

Library of Congress Cataloging-in-Publication Data

Miller, Charles Edward, 1929-
    As rain that falls: homiletic reflections for the weekdays of
Advent & Lent / by Charles E. Miller.
        p. 158   cm. 14 × 21
    ISBN 0-8189-0535-2
    1. Advent sermons.   2. Lenten sermons.   3. Catholic Church—
Sermons.   4. Sermons, American.   I. Title.
BX1756.M554A7   1988
252'.61—dc19   88-13963
                                                                          CIP

Imprimi Potest:
Jerome R. Herff, C.M.
Provincial, Province of the West

Nihil Obstat:
Newman C. Eberhardt, C.M.
Censor deputatus

Imprimatur:
Roger M. Mahony
Archbishop of Los Angeles
January 25, 1988

Designed, printed and bound in the United States of
America by the Fathers and Brothers of the
Society of St. Paul, 2187 Victory Boulevard,
Staten Island, New York 10314, as part of their
communications apostolate.

Printing Information:

Current Printing - first digit 1 2 3 4 5 6 7 8 9 10 11 12 13 14 15 16 17 18 19 20

Year of Current Printing - first year shown
1988   1989   1990   1991   1992   1993   1994   1995   1996   1997   1998   1999

AS RAIN THAT FALLS

Homiletic Reflections for the Weekdays of Advent and Lent

Charles E. Miller, C.M.

"Just as from the heavens
the rain and the snow come down
And do not return there
till they have watered the earth,
making it fertile and fruitful,
Giving seed to him who sows
and bread to him who eats,
So shall my word be
that goes forth from my mouth;
It shall not return to me void,
but shall do my will,
achieving the end for which I sent it."

(Isaiah 55:10-11)

"O thou Lord of life, send my roots rain."

Gerard Manley Hopkins

"By means of the homily
the mysteries of the faith and
the guiding principles of the Christian life
are expounded from the sacred text
during the course of the liturgical year.
The homily, therefore, is to be highly esteemed
as part of the liturgy itself."

(*Constitution on the Sacred Liturgy*, 52)

PREFACE

This book is not a collection of homilies. Words on a page are not a homily. A homily is a live, oral presentation which is an integral part of a liturgical celebration. I prefer to call these compositions "homiletic reflections." They are reflections on the sacred scripture in a homiletic style, drawn from the weekdays of Advent and Lent when the Church urges that a homily be preached each day.

For those who use this book as a source of personal meditation, I hope that it will help them to grow in a life of greater love, prayer, and service. For those who are charged with the sublime duty of preaching, I hope that it will be a stimulus for them to compose and proclaim their own homiletic presentations of the Word.

The Word proclaimed and heard is like the rain from the heavens. Only God gives the fruitfulness. May he grant us all the gift of a hundredfold.

"By your gift I will utter praise in the vast assembly" (Psalm 22:26).

"Advent has a twofold character. It is
a time of preparation for Christmas when the first coming
of God's Son to his people is recalled.
It is also a season when minds are directed
by this memorial to
Christ's second coming at the end of time.
It is thus a season of joyful
and spiritual expectation"

(*Norms for the Liturgical Year and Calendar*, 39)

Part One

THE FIRST THREE WEEKS
OF ADVENT

MONDAY OF THE FIRST WEEK OF ADVENT (I)

Advent is a time of preparation. It is intended to get us ready both for Christmas, the first coming of Christ, and for what is called the parousia, his second coming.

A question to be posed is whether we can be optimistic about the second coming. An answer is derived, not from thinking about the future, but from looking to the past.

Our faith and hope in God are not based on abstract notions of his goodness but on a witness to his actions. That witness comes to us from the teaching of the Church in her scriptures and her tradition. We reflect on the actions of God in the past because we believe that God is consistent. You can depend on him. What God has done, God will do.

Did Jesus listen to the plea of the centurion? Then he will listen to our prayers. Did Jesus free the centurion's servant from his painful paralysis which left him helpless? Then Jesus will free us from the paralysis of sin which prevents us from advancing toward God and our heavenly home.

During the season of Advent daily Mass will present important selections from sacred scripture. Through these readings we will see that all of God's actions show his wisdom and love. We can depend on this good and wise God to prepare us to share in the glory of Christ when he comes again.

MONDAY OF THE FIRST WEEK OF ADVENT (II)

During Advent we will be hearing many readings from the prophet Isaiah. If we could have met Isaiah in person, it is likely that we would have been awed by him.

Isaiah's writings suggest that he was a man of great dignity. Although there is no evidence that he was of royal blood, he moved amid kings and princes with ease and confidence, and he never hesitated to admonish any official of the court. Despite his dignity he was not above walking the streets of Jerusalem barefoot and clad only in a loin cloth, like an ancient Gandhi, to dramatize the folly of trusting in political pacts rather than in God.

Isaiah's contemporaries were preoccupied with the military threat of Assyria, the Russia of his day. During his lifetime he saw the northern kingdom of Israel conquered by the Assyrians and his own land of Judah invaded. But Isaiah was primarily concerned about the spiritual attitude of his people. He lamented the fact that they preferred to trust in arms and alliances rather than in God.

Isaiah urged his nation to beat its swords into plowshares and its spears into pruning hooks. He longed for a day when weapons of war would be transformed into instruments of peace. The message of Isaiah was not easy for his people to hear, nor is it easy for us. But listen we must during Advent, for Isaiah's words truly are the Word of the Lord.

TUESDAY OF THE FIRST WEEK OF ADVENT (I)

No scene in all of Christian history is more tender and endearing than that of the crib in Bethlehem. Blest are our eyes of faith as we look at a mere infant and recognize the eternal Son of God. What God has hidden from the learned and the clever, he has revealed to us, his children.

There were great people of the Old Testament before Christ was born: Abraham, our father in faith, Moses, the great lawgiver, and David, the royal ancestor of the Messiah-King. And yet they were not afforded the revelation granted to us, that God so loved the world that in the fullness of time he sent his only Son to be our Savior.

Wonderful though Christmas is, there is something still more wonderful to come. Christmas shows us that God was born in humility, but he will come again in glory. At Bethlehem we see a helpless infant, but at the end of the world we will see Christ come in power and might.

We have good reason to wait in joyful hope for the coming of our Savior, Jesus Christ, for our eyes will be blest to see that the kingdom, the power, and the glory are his, now and forever.

TUESDAY OF THE FIRST WEEK OF ADVENT (II)

A great theme of Advent is that God is at work to transform the humble and the lowly. That is why we are asked to think about the coming of God as a child, an infant. No one is more humble than a little child, and no one, in a sense, is poorer than an infant since he has nothing to call his own. And yet a baby is a sign of hope.

Think of the marvel of human growth. Seven or eight pounds of cuddly humanity with loving care becomes transformed into the fullness of adulthood. That is a symbol of God's advent. He transforms the lowly. God transformed David's dynasty, no more than a stump in the forest, into the marvel of the messianic kingdom.

It happens everyday at Mass. What could be more lowly or more simple than a little bread and some inexpensive wine? And yet God transforms these elements into a marvelous gift for us, the body and the blood of his divine Son.

With this coming of the Lord in the eucharist we, too, are being transformed. That which happens to an infant, and that which happens to the bread and the wine, will happen in its own way for us and the entire universe when Christ comes again.

WEDNESDAY OF THE FIRST WEEK OF ADVENT (I)

One of the greatest needs we have as human beings is nourishment. We simply cannot grow or even survive without food and drink.

Human need for nourishment brought forth from Jesus some of the most tender signs of his compassion.

When Jesus saw the people in today's gospel, he said to the apostles, "My heart is moved with pity for the crowd. By now they have been with me three days and they have nothing to eat. I do not wish to send them away hungry."

People who are really hungry can think of little but food, and they become preoccupied with getting something to eat. When the Son of God became human like us, he accepted all aspects of our lives, including the feeling of hunger. He knew from his own human experience how the crowd felt.

It should not surprise us, then, that Jesus responded to the need of the people by working a miracle for them. What should absolutely amaze us is that Jesus responds to our spiritual hunger in a way which is greater than a miracle. When we come to him in prayer at Mass, he does not wish to send us away hungry. He nourishes us with his body and blood in the holy eucharist. The eucharist is a wonderful gift which Jesus in his compassion gives to us every day. Would that this food could become our preoccupation!

WEDNESDAY OF THE FIRST WEEK OF ADVENT (II)

Civilized people have transformed the animal necessity of eating and drinking into a human experience.

Dining is different from eating alone at a fast food establishment. We come together not only to seek nourishment but to express relationships and to celebrate events. Peace and relaxation should characterize the event. Arguing and bickering during a meal not only upset the digestion but mar the beauty of what sharing a meal should mean.

It is not surprising that the prophet Isaiah envisioned a glorious future for God's people as a banquet: "a feast of rich food and choice wines." Jesus too used the image of a grand dinner, especially a wedding banquet, to visualize the messianic era.

As a people of hope we look toward the second coming of Christ when he will bring to completion his kingdom of justice, love, and peace. As we wait for that moment and prepare for it, we should remember that Jesus has transformed our human experience of eating and drinking into a liturgical celebration of our relationship with him. He gives us his body and blood as our spiritual food and drink. Sharing in the eucharist will fill us with the joy of Christ now and prepare us to share in his eternal kingdom of justice, love, and peace.

THURSDAY OF THE FIRST WEEK OF ADVENT (I)

To do God's will is the indispensable sign of our love for him. Dedication to God's will is the measure of true devotion.

The human life of Jesus began within the atmosphere of dedication to God's will. At the time of the Annunciation, Mary said, "Be it done to me according to your word," and in that moment when she embraced the Father's will, Jesus was conceived in her womb.

The human life of Jesus ended with his dedication to his Father's will. During his agony in the garden on the night of his passion, he prayed, "Father, not my will, but yours be done." The next day he died on the cross in accord with his dedication when he said, "Father, into your hands I commend my spirit."

At Mass Jesus invites us to join him in his prayer to the Father: "Thy will be done." But words are not enough. Actions are needed. That is why Jesus tells us, "None of those who cry out, 'Lord, Lord,' will enter the kingdom of God but only the one who does the will of my Father in heaven."

Parents understand this teaching. Children are not obedient who say, "Yes, I will do my homework," but then go outside and play.

Life is too serious and full of meaning to waste it by playing games with God. We are wise to build our lives on dedication to God's will.

THURSDAY OF THE FIRST WEEK OF ADVENT (II)

Once a little child has experienced Christmas, he never asks, *"Will* Santa Claus come?" only *"When* will he come?" There is a wisdom in experience, even in that of a child, and that wisdom leads to trust. Trust is the rock, the foundation, of which Jesus speaks in the gospel today.

Isaiah exhorted the people, "Trust in the Lord forever." But why should they trust in the Lord? Because of his deeds, because he had saved them in the Exodus and formed them into his people with whom he made a covenant. Isaiah was saying, "You can depend on God." What God has done, that God will do.

The Opening Prayer of today's Mass contains a simple plea, "Father, we need your help." This is not an expression of desperation. It is a prayer of trust. It is based on the truth that God sent his Son into our world to free us from sin and to form us into his people with whom he made a covenant in the blood of his Son.

When we pray, it is reasonable that we ask, "Father, *when* will you help us?" To ask "when" is a sign of faith, not doubt. The only question we must never ask is *"Will* God help us?" Wisdom says, "You can depend on God," and this wisdom leads to trust, the foundation of our lives.

FRIDAY OF THE FIRST WEEK OF ADVENT (I)

When Jesus cured the two blind men, he showed great compassion. But there was more to this miracle than compassion. It was one in a series of signs which pointed to the identity of Jesus as the Messiah.

Later in the gospel some of the disciples of John the Baptist came to Jesus and asked, "Are you the one who is to come, or should we look for another?" Jesus replied, "The blind regain their sight, the lame walk, lepers are cleansed, the deaf hear, the dead are raised, and the poor have the good news proclaimed to them." That was his answer about his identity.

The two blind men appreciated what Jesus had done for them. We trust that with open eyes they recognized who Jesus is and embraced him as their Savior.

Our eyes were opened in baptism. We were given a special vision called faith. With the eyes of faith, we need to observe carefully all that Jesus does for us. We are cleansed of the leprosy of sin. We are not deaf to the good news which is proclaimed to us; we hear the Word of God. We have been raised from the death of sin and given new life in Christ. We walk strong and sure in the light of Christ.

Are we to look for another than Jesus? Certainly not. He is our Savior and Lord.

FRIDAY OF THE FIRST WEEK OF ADVENT (II)

When Isaiah wrote of a future age, he put a strong emphasis on light and vision. Today's reading declares that the blind will see, and at midnight Mass we will hear Isaiah say in the first reading: "The people who walked in darkness have seen a great light."

That light is the gift of faith. It was given to us in our baptism. The priest presented a candle and said, "Receive the light of Christ." Then he prayed that we might keep the flame of faith alive in our hearts.

Faith is the foundation of our lives as disciples of Christ. Imagine life without faith. We would not know God and his great love. Christmas would be meaningless and the crucifixion would look like a failure. Mary would be an unknown Jewish girl who lived and died like all other girls in her village. We would not know and love her as the mother of God and our mother. Without faith we would have no Church, no eucharist, no hope for eternal life.

But Jesus has cured us of spiritual blindness as surely as he cured the two blind men in the gospel. Faith is his Christmas gift to us.

SATURDAY OF THE FIRST WEEK OF ADVENT (I)

The human heart of Jesus was moved with pity for the crowd. He saw them as sheep without a shepherd.

We know that Jesus is the Good Shepherd, and yet today's gospel shows that Jesus wanted the apostles to be shepherds too. He sent the twelve as shepherds, and to them he said, "The gift you have received, give as a gift."

There is more to our relationship with Christ than being on the receiving end. He wants us to share his shepherding by giving to others the gifts we have received. For that purpose we need to reflect on our gifts.

Your gift may be compassion. When you see someone in need, perhaps a neighbor who is sick, your heart is moved with pity and you offer your services. Your gift may be a willingness to pay attention to a person who really wants someone to listen. Your gift may be that you have sufficient funds to help the poor financially and to contribute to charitable causes.

We ought to realize that whenever we help someone, we are actually giving the gift of Christ himself. Ultimately any talent or possession we have shares in the person of Christ, and so in helping others we are giving the gift of Christ himself. In being loving and generous in any way, we make Christ come alive. We become a continual advent so that Christ is always having a new birth in our world.

SATURDAY OF THE FIRST WEEK OF ADVENT (II)

Thomas Jefferson formulated a great truth when he wrote that the Creator has endowed us with "the rights to life, liberty, and the pursuit of happiness."

And *pursue* happiness is what we do. Happiness is elusive, like wet soap which keeps slipping through our hands and falling to the floor of the shower.

When Isaiah wished to assure the people of God's blessings, he said: "The Lord will give you the bread you need and the water for which you thirst." Isaiah used the metaphor of nourishment to suggest those things which are necessary for human existence and which make it pleasant.

But God is more than a provider. It is not what God gives that will make us happy. It is God himself. We must yearn for God more intensely than a person who is dying of thirst yearns for water.

Although we possess God on this earth, we are a people who are on a journey to God's home where we will be filled by him. From the proper direction we must not deviate: no side trips and no turning and walking in the opposite direction. Listening to the sacred scriptures at Mass, and meditating on them at home, will guide us. Being open to God's word will keep us on the right road. When we would turn to the right or to the left, a voice shall sound in our ears, "This is the way; walk in it."

MONDAY OF THE SECOND WEEK OF ADVENT (I)

Throughout human history God has been willing, even eager, to forgive the repentant sinner. We believe that is true because of our faith in God's mercy. And yet after the coming of Jesus the forgiveness of sins took on a new, human expression which leads to certitude.

Jesus forgave the sins of the paralytic through human words: "My friend, your sins are forgiven." When the Pharisees objected to this manner of forgiveness, Jesus responded with a humanly discernible sign: he cured the paralytic through his words to show that he could forgive sins through his words. The words, "Your sins are forgiven" are just as powerful as "Stand up and walk."

In faith we believe tha: ı the sacrament of penance, Jesus continues to forgive sins. H. ıs present in the human words of the priest: "I absolve you from your sins."

Some people ask, "But ¬an't God forgive my sins, even terrible ones, when I pray tc ıim directly for mercy?" The answer is that God can do whatever he wants. But God normally forgives serious sins through the sacrament of penance. The marvel of this sacrament is that we hear human words, incarnate words, which assure us of forgiveness. Such is one of the blessings of the birth of the Son of God into our world.

MONDAY OF THE SECOND WEEK OF ADVENT (II)

Wise people say things like, "Take each day at a time. Live for the present. The past is gone and the future is not here yet."

And yet there is within the human heart an incurable instinct to look for something better in the future. Never try telling a child not to look forward to Christmas. When a child asks, "How many more days until Christmas?" it won't work to say, "Don't worry about it." Not ten minutes later the child will ask again, "How many more days until Christmas?"

Hoping for a better future is part of faith, whether a person is an Israelite in slavery in Babylon or a paralytic in Judah. Nor is our hope without foundation. That is why the prophet Isaiah declares, "Say to those whose hearts are frightened: Be strong, fear not." And Jesus says, "Take courage; your sins are forgiven."

We experience marvels which should give us strength and courage in looking to the future: Jesus frees us from sin which alone can paralyze and discourage us; Jesus gives us strength through the nourishment of his body and blood.

Advent strikes a responsive chord within us because Advent mirrors life. Life is always "not quite" and "not yet." There is always more needed, something still to come. But Christian expectation is rooted in a sound hope, and that hope should give us confidence about the future.

TUESDAY OF THE SECOND WEEK OF ADVENT (I)

In the early Church the favorite representation of Christ was
that of the Good Shepherd. This image pictured the love and
care which Jesus manifests for all his people. It still has an effect
upon us today many centuries later, even though our
experience with shepherding may be rare.

Even granting the dedication of a shepherd to his sheep,
today's gospel may evoke a somewhat skeptical response.
Would a shepherd really leave ninety-nine sheep out on the
hills and go in search of the single stray sheep? Although he
could safely leave the ninety-nine for a short time since sheep
are gregarious and do not tend to scatter, the question still
remains.

Jesus does not imply that that one person is equal in value
to one hundred; God does not deal in mathematical values.
Rather the point is that the shepherd must not abandon a single
sheep because it is only one. Just before telling the parable,
Jesus warned his disciples, "See that you never despise one of
the little ones." Just after the parable he added, "It is no part of
your heavenly Father's plan that a single one of these little ones
shall ever come to grief."

We are the little ones, precious in the eyes of God,
searched out and embraced by the Good Shepherd. Jesus asks
us, "What is your thought on this?"

TUESDAY OF THE SECOND WEEK OF ADVENT (II)

The prophet Isaiah lived about seven hundred years before the birth of Christ. Although his ministry was limited to the city of Jerusalem, his influence spread, and he developed devoted disciples who continued his mission after his death.
These disciples helped to compile the sixty-six chapters of the book in the Bible which we call the Book of Isaiah.

Today's reading is the beginning of the Second Part of Isaiah, composed approximately one hundred and fifty years after his death, and addressed to the people who were exiled in the Babylonian captivity. True to the spirit of Isaiah, this Second Part begins on an optimistic note. It is a message of comfort which assures the exiles that their captivity is at an end because God has not abandoned his people. God is a true shepherd who feeds his flock and leads them home.

We are a people in exile. As wonderful as this world is, we are here only for a time. Heaven is our home. In the prayer known as "The Hail Holy Queen" (or *Salve Regina*), we say to Mary, "After this our exile, show unto us the blessed fruit of your womb, Jesus."

Mary, we can be sure, knew and dearly loved the Book of Isaiah. In his spirit she says to us, "Take comfort. My Son, the Good Shepherd, feeds you with his body and blood to strengthen you on your journey home."

WEDNESDAY OF THE SECOND WEEK OF ADVENT (I)

We really ought to be very happy to hear the words of Jesus in today's gospel: "Come to me, all you who are weary and find life burdensome, and I will refresh you."

Jesus is unlike even our most cherished fellow human beings. We don't have to wonder whether Jesus is in a good mood. We don't have to worry that he may misunderstand something we have to say. We don't even have to ask whether he is too busy for us today.

Jesus is available without fail. He is always eager to embrace us. We can visit him in the Blessed Sacrament whenever we drop into church, and we can listen to him in the pages of sacred scripture. Above all else he refreshes us at Mass with the precious gift of his body and his blood.

But we must never think of Jesus as being confined to any one place or to a single manner of presence. He is with us when we sleep, and he is with us when we awake. He is with us when we work, and he is with us when we play. He is with us when we are alone, and he is with us when we are in the company of others.

Jesus will never force himself upon us. The decision to accept his invitation or to reject it is our own.

WEDNESDAY OF THE SECOND WEEK OF ADVENT (II)

The great virtue of Advent is hope. It is a time for us to grow in trust, to learn to put our lives completely in the hands of the Lord and to believe that he will always do what is best for us.

I he people to whom today's first reading was addressed are far removed from us in time and circumstances. What we have in common with them is the call to trust in the Lord, no matter how bleak matters may seem.

When the people were exiles during the Babylonian captivity, they came close to despair. They felt abandoned by God. They even began to doubt his power to save them.

The exiles were at a point of crisis when the prophet called them to remember who the Lord is. He is not like the stars which their pagan masters worshipped; rather, he is the creator of the heavens and all they contain. He is not restricted by the limits of time and space; rather, he is the eternal God who does not grow weary. He is not searching for the best way to conduct the business of the world; rather, his knowledge is beyond scrutiny.

The Lord is unique and not to be compared with the pagan gods who reflect human weaknesses. In short, there is no one to whom the Lord can be likened as an equal.

The Lord is worthy of our trust; hope in him is never misplaced.

THURSDAY OF THE SECOND WEEK OF AC √ENT (I)

During our Advent liturgies a strange figure emerges from the pages of the gospel. He is John the Baptist, an eccentric person whose clothing was camel's hair and whose food was grasshoppers.

I suspect that if we had met the Baptist in person many of us would not have been inclined to invite him to dinner, not because we would have no idea of how to prepare grasshoppers, but because we would have felt uncomfortable in his presence. And yet Jesus declared that history has not known a man born of woman greater than John the Baptist.

As we listen to John's message during Advent we will find that we are looking beyond the sweet, touching scene of the crib to see Jesus, not as a helpless infant, but as a grown man.

There is good reason for an emphasis on Jesus as an adult even as we prepare for his birth. The liturgy is concerned with the incomprehensible truth that God became human, but even more emphatically the liturgy proclaims the reason why he became human. As a grown man Jesus opened his arms on the cross for the salvation of the world.

Perhaps some feel as uncomfortable in thinking about the crucifixion as they would about inviting John the Baptist to dinner. But the crib led to the cross. Bethlehem was fulfilled on Calvary. Our Advent is incomplete without an appreciation of the sacrifice of the cross.

THURSDAY OF THE SECOND WEEK OF ADVENT (II)

The people in exile during the Babylonian captivity were miserable. They felt like insignificant worms in contrast to their enemies who seemed like mighty mountains. They thought of themselves as demeaned as maggots feeding in filth in contrast to their captors who dined in elegance.

The word of the Lord to these people was simple: "Fear not, I will help you." It is a word meant for us as well. We should never think of ourselves as worms or maggots, but we ought to realize that God favors those who are simple, even lowly, in human estimation.

Jesus helps us to learn the lesson. He "emptied himself and took the form of a slave, being born in human likeness. He humbled himself, becoming obedient unto death, even death on a cross" (Philippians 2:7-8). In his crucifixion he fulfilled the words of the psalm, "I am a worm, not a man; the scorn of men, despised by the people" (Psalm 22:6).

As surely as he raised Jesus from the dead, so will God help his humble, simple people in their needs. We have signs of this truth at Mass. In the liturgy our prayers, insignificant in themselves, became as mighty as mountains. We do more than dine in elegance. We are nourished with the body and blood of Christ.

The Lord means it when he says, "Fear not; I will help you."

FRIDAY OF THE SECOND WEEK OF ADVENT (I)

Some people find fault with everything. They are never pleased with the movies they see and they are never satisfied with the dinners they eat. When it comes to religion, they do not abandon their criticial spirit.

The episode in today's gospel suggests that Jesus was frustrated with just such people. They judged that John the Baptist was possessed by a demon because he neither ate nor drank, and they accused Jesus of being a glutton and a drunkard because he dined with tax collectors and those outside the law.

If the critical people had humbly opened themselves to the wisdom of the Spirit, they would have seen the meaning both of the penitential preaching of John the Baptist and the joyous proclamation of Jesus.

The practice of the penance preached by John leads to the joy of the forgiveness proclaimed by Jesus.

John's role was one of preparation for the coming of Jesus just as the practice of penance is a preparation for full Christian living. When our sins are washed away, we are flooded with the love of God. God dwells within us as in a temple. A Benedictine monk, Abbot Columba Marmion, wrote that "joy is the echo of God's life within us."

During Advent we reflect on the truth that God so loved the world that he sent his only Son to be our Savior. Wisdom tells us that this is a cause, not for grief, but for joy.

FRIDAY OF THE SECOND WEEK OF ADVENT (II)

Many years ago Frank Sheed, an English layman, wrote a book called *A Map of Life*. The title aptly suggests that in this world we are on a journey, that we are a pilgrim people.

If you are trying to find some location in a foreign country, there are three approaches. You can trust your instincts and hope you are going in the right direction. You can ask people for directions. You can follow a map.

The first approach works if you happen to be lucky enough to have chosen the right direction, but it usually ends in failure. The second works if you ask informed people for guidance. The third works if the map is correct.

The people addressed in today's first reading had drifted away from the right path. They had made two basic mistakes. They had trusted their own inclinations, which happened to be wrong, and they had followed the example of their pagan neighbors, who did not know where they were going in life. As a result the people ended in exile in Babylonia.

God reminded them that he had given them the right people to listen to about life, the prophets, and had even provided them with a map of life, his commandments. He said: "I, the Lord, your God, teach you what is for your good and lead you on the way you should go."

Do we not have the same advantage?

SATURDAY OF THE SECOND WEEK OF ADVENT (I)

Elijah was one of the holiest persons of the Old Testament. So holy was he that a tradition developed to the effect that he did not die, but that God, so to speak, sent a chariot to swing low and carry him home. But Elijah's mission was not ended when he left this earth. It had to be completed in the person of John the Baptist.

Jesus has gone before us and been taken to heaven in glory. But his mission has not ended. He wants to continue his ministry in each one of his disciples. This ministry may be taking communion to and caring for the sick. It may be working to secure human rights. It may be the ministry of prayer for those in special need. Whatever may be the activity of our ministry, we need to realize that ultimately mission is not primarily doing something, but being someone. Ministry means being Christ to the world.

When Jesus calls us to his ministry, he gives us the means to carry it out. That means is the eucharist, the sacrament of transformation into Christ.

Each day should be an Advent in which we long for and prepare for that moment when we celebrate the eucharist together and open ourselves to the power of Christ. In the eucharist Jesus swings low to catch us up, not in a chariot, but in his arms so that his ministry may continue in this world.

SATURDAY OF THE SECOND WEEK OF ADVENT (II)

A tradition developed among the Jews that the prophet Elijah would return to earth to prepare for the coming of the Messiah. One reason some people did not accept Jesus as the Christ is that, in their view, Elijah had not yet appeared as his herald.

The answer is that Elijah had come in the person of John the Baptist. This answer is not based on an idea of reincarnation as if Elijah were inhabiting the body of John the Baptist. Rather both Elijah and John the Baptist were seen as personifications of the people with whom God had made a covenant. It was their destiny to be the source of the Messiah.

Christ is the center of history. All that went before him prepared for his coming. The people and their covenant with God, the prophets and their teachings about God, all led up to the life, death, and resurrection of Jesus Christ. Now everything flows from Christ and his mission on earth.

Christ is not only the center of history but its focus. He sharpens our vision of God. He makes clear the meaning and purpose of human existence. He makes distinct our ideas of what is right and wrong.

The message of Advent is: keep your eyes fixed on Christ. Let him be the person who is the center of your whole being. Let his teaching and life give meaning and purpose to your existence.

MONDAY OF THE THIRD WEEK OF ADVENT (I)

The leaders of the people demanded to hear from Jesus why he presumed to preach in the temple precincts. After all, in their view he was nothing more than an itinerant preacher without credentials.

Jesus did not answer their demand. He countered with a question to which he knew the leaders could not respond. Jesus did not wish to engage in an argument. He wanted the leaders to realize that there were more mysteries in the kingdom of God than they realized, and that faith, not polemics, was needed.

Underlying the entire situation was the supposition that Jesus was nothing more than he appeared to be. We have been led by God beyond the world of suppositions and appearances into that of revelation. In faith we accept Jesus as more than human; we believe that he is the divine and eternal Son of God.

This faith in the divinity of Jesus is behind all of our Advent preparations for his coming. If Jesus were no more than human, why bother? Even the most avid patriot of our country does not spend four weeks, or even four days, in preparing for the birthday of George Washington.

Christmas is more than a birthday. It is a testimony to God's incomprehensible love which moved him to send his beloved Son to be our Savior.

MONDAY OF THE THIRD WEEK OF ADVENT (II)

Today's reading from the Book of Numbers reminds us that we cannot limit how or where God will work.

When the Israelites were on their way from Egypt to the promised land, the Moabite king feared that they would take over his country. He sent Balaam, a pagan seer, to curse the Israelites and so render them powerless. But God would not permit Balaam even to utter the words of a curse. Each time he tried, his words turned into a blessing.

The Israelites were shocked. They did not believe that God would be at work in a pagan. And yet their realization that God spoke through Balaam did not in any way lessen their appreciation of their own identity as God's special people.

Some have erroneously thought that ecumenism means that all religions are the same and they fear that Catholics have lost a sense of the value of being a Catholic.

The Second Vatican Council, not surprisingly, has a perfectly balanced teaching on the subject. In the Dogmatic Constitution on the Church, the Council teaches: "The Church of Christ subsists in the Catholic Church, although many elements of sanctification and of truth can be found outside of her visible structure. These elements, however, as gifts which properly belong to the Church of Christ possess an inner dynamism toward Catholic unity" (#8).

We cannot limit how or where God will work.

TUESDAY OF THE THIRD WEEK OF ADVENT (I)

Jesus liked to teach by drawing on human nature. The story of the two sons shows how well Jesus understood people. Some children say they will be obedient but go ahead and do whatever they want; others grumble but eventually follow their parents' wishes.

Jesus told the parable to justify his favor toward those who were held in contempt by some of the religious leaders. These people, though beginning by rejecting God's will, repented and found favor. The leaders, on the other hand, mouthed platitudes about following God's law but really made themselves the law. Jesus taught that words are not obedience; actions are.

Jesus understands us and knows how hard it is for us to abandon our self-love and to embrace God's will. But he wants more than words from us. In addition to saying in the Lord's prayer, "Thy will be done," we must follow the example of Jesus.

Although Jesus was divine, he became human like us in all things but sin, and his human obedience to the will of his Father led him to death on the cross. Was that easy for Jesus? Certainly not. In fact, as he suffered in the garden on the night before he was to die, he almost sounded like the son who said, "I will not go." But from his prayer Jesus found the strength to say to his Father, "Not my will, but yours be done." And he followed that will to the cross.

TUESDAY OF THE THIRD WEEK OF ADVENT (II)

In almost every era there are prophets of doom. Sometimes their pessimism is warranted. The prophet Zephaniah clearly had reason to proclaim a dire message. He lived in the decadent times of the seventh century before Christ when the city of Jerusalem had rebelled against God and had turned to the worship of false deities. As the people abandoned God, they became guilty of grave social injustice.

To the corrupt city Zephaniah proclaimed impending judgment. But the picture was not entirely dark. The Lord promised that he would spare a holy remnant who would remain faithful to him.

We read this prophecy during Advent because it was through this remnant that the Savior was born into our world. They are one of the human links in the chain which led to the first coming of Christ.

We do not need a prophet to paint a bleak picture of our society with its worship of the false gods of individualism and self-love which lead to social injustices. But even in the dark there remains a ray of light. God calls us to be his remnant.

If we are to love God, we cannot ignore people and their needs. We are called to live lives of unselfish love, to overcome the temptation to be preoccupied with our own pleasures. We are invited to be one of the links which will lead to the day when Christ will come again to establish his kingdom of justice, love, and peace.

WEDNESDAY OF THE THIRD WEEK OF ADVENT (I)

The people in exile began to have doubts about God. Their doubts did not center around God's existence; atheism was, in their view, an absurd opinion. Since they were surrounded by pagans who believed in a multiplicity of gods, they were tempted to compare their God with those of the pagans. They wondered how powerful their God, the Lord, really was.

God, replying through his prophet, did not appeal to his might. He did not brag, so to speak, about how much greater he was than all of the pagan gods. He did not, in fact, use the comparative degree at all since there really is no one with whom he can compare himself.

The Lord declared quite simply: "I am God; there is no other." And since the Lord alone is God, the prophet told the people that they must trust him: "In the Lord shall be the vindication and the glory of all the descendants of Israel."

Spiritually we are those descendants. Because of the revelation granted to us, we have a deeper understanding of monotheism. We believe that there is one God, but we all believe that in the one God are three persons. The second person, the eternal Son of God, became man and was born into our world. He is our vindication, for through him the guilt of our sins has been wiped away. He is our glory, for through him we have received a share in the eternal life of God.

WEDNESDAY OF THE THIRD WEEK OF ADVENT (II)

Doubts can enter into human relationships. Some misunderstanding develops into a fear that there has been a cooling of affection. A need to be alone leads to a suspicion that someone else has taken first place. Questions are asked but they have the ring of accusation.

Such seems to be the situation in today's gospel. John the Baptist had already proclaimed Jesus to be the awaited Messiah. Why did he now send his disciples to ask the question, "Are you 'He who is to come,' or do we look for someone else?"

The question has a ring of an accusation to it. John was languishing in prison. He wanted to know how that could be. What was wrong with Jesus? Didn't he realize that as the Messiah he should come with the might of God's wrath and crush all opposition?

Jesus replied by pointing out that his role was to bring to the oppressed and downtrodden the blessings proclaimed in the Book of Isaiah. His kingdom is one of justice, love, and peace. It comes about in God's own way, not by force but through invitation.

At times we may want to ask God why he is not doing things our way. We do not doubt his power but we are disappointed that he is not using that power on our behalf. What is wrong with him? Doesn't he know that he is God? Yes, he is God and that is precisely why things must be done his way.

THURSDAY OF THE THIRD WEEK OF ADVENT (I)

John the Baptist was a great man. It is somewhat surprising, therefore, to hear Jesus declare that the least born into the kingdom of God is greater than he.

The point is hardly that John was not born into the kingdom of God. The point is that all the wonderful qualities of John—his self-denial, his dedication to prayer, his role as the prophet who introduced the Messiah—are actually less important than being part of God's kingdom. If you were to consider these qualities apart from John's being part of the kingdom, the least born into the kingdom of God is indeed greater than he.

Everybody wants to be important. Some people talk constantly about themselves, or boast about their beautiful car, or even brag about the accomplishments of their children. All of this is done in an attempt to appear important.

Appearances do not matter. What is significant is not what we have done, but what God has done for us. He thought we were so important that he sent his only Son to be our Savior. Jesus could have appeared as some kind of extraordinary creature from outer space. Instead, in order to enhance the dignity of our race, already ennobled by having been created in the image of God, he became human like us in all things but sin.

There are the favors heaped upon those born into the kingdom of God through faith and baptism. In God's eyes we are all VIP's.

THURSDAY OF THE THIRD WEEK OF ADVENT (II)

We learn by going from the known to the unknown. Even the Bible follows this process in helping us to learn about God and his relationship with us.

One of the Bible's favorite points of comparison in both the Old and the New Testaments is marriage. The relationship between God and his people is like that between spouses. Usually the Bible wants to emphasize love, fidelity, and fruitfulness as qualities of our relationship with God. Today's reading from Isaiah, however, reflects certain realities of married love which are not pleasant.

The fact is that between spouses there are misunderstandings. Sometimes harsh arguments follow. Disgruntlement can be so severe that it leads to estrangement, and estrangement to infidelity.

Israel had been unfaithful to God despite his great love for her. In the exile during captivity in Babylon the people were like a deserted wife, barren and desolate.

Now comes a reality which transcends human reactions. A human spouse quite understandably has a limit. But God says to the people, "With great tenderness I will take you back. Though the mountains leave their place and the hills be shaken, my love shall never leave you."

These are indeed beautiful words, and they are addressed to us as well as to the people of the exile. God's love for us is not only visualized through this Old Testament passage; it comes alive for us in the person of his Son who was born as our Savior.

FRIDAY OF THE THIRD WEEK OF ADVENT (I)

Pope John XXIII liked to emphasize that we need to read the signs of the times (cf. his encyclical *Pacem in Terris*). Anyone who does not realize that Christmas is coming has not been reading the signs of the month of December. Even the most disinterested person must admit that Christmas will soon be here.

Jesus expected the people of his day to be aware of what he had been doing, to read the signs. He said: "The works which I perform testify on my behalf that the Father has sent me."

Even though we await the coming of Christ in glory, he expects us to be aware of what is going on around us now. The truth is that Christ, though yet to come in glory at the end of time, is still being sent by the Father into our world. He is among us. We see the signs of Christmas with the eyes of our body; we see Christ around us with the eyes of our faith.

The Second Vatican Council in its Constitution on the Sacred Liturgy (#7) urges us to be aware of the presence of Christ in four particular ways. He is present where two or three are gathered in his name, as people come together for the liturgy. He is present in the Word proclaimed at Mass. He is present in the priest. And preeminently he is present in the holy eucharist. We must not miss the signs of his presence.

FRIDAY OF THE THIRD WEEK OF ADVENT (II)

The Jews were surrounded by people who believed in a multiplicity of gods. Some thought that each nation had its own god. In fact, when nations went to war, the understanding was that one god was struggling to overcome the other god.

The Jews were blessed with the revelation that there is but one God. Even though they fell into polytheism from time to time, their main problem was that they tended to become possessive of the Lord, viewing him as their God alone who was not to be shared with other peoples.

Today's reading from the Book of Isaiah is strong in its emphasis against this form of particularism. The Lord did not want those who were not Jewish to think that he would exclude them from his people. In a beautiful expression of universalism God proclaimed through his prophet: "My house shall be called a house of prayer for all peoples."

We are those people who have been invited into the house of the Lord. We do so with the realization that the God of Israel is the God of Christians, and that since there is but one Lord there should be harmony among all his many people.

The song of the Christmas angels proclaimed peace, but peace comes about only when people are willing to cooperate with each other in mutual respect. An authentic Christmas spirit excludes no one from our attention, our concern, and our prayers.

"Within the cycle of a year
the Church unfolds the whole mystery of Christ,
not only from his incarnation and birth
until his ascension, but also
as reflected in the day of Pentecost,
and the expectation of a blessed,
hoped-for return of the Lord."

(Constitution on the Sacred Liturgy, 102)

Part Two

DECEMBER 17th THROUGH
DECEMBER 24th

DECEMBER 17th (I)

Most people have been getting ready for Christmas for weeks, and smart shoppers have done their buying early to make sure they had the pick of the items they wanted.

God prepared for the first Christmas over a period, not of weeks or even years, but of centuries. He started a long time ago and was very careful about choosing people who would be part of his gift giving.

This time of preparation, the history of our salvation, began with Abraham. God made promises to Abraham which were without condition. The covenant with Abraham was unilateral; it all depended on God. The Messiah came in fulfillment of this covenant.

With Abraham, a narrowing down process began. Abraham had a son Isaac. Isaac had a son Jacob. And Jacob had twelve sons, the fathers of the twelve tribes of Israel. From among these tribes God chose the tribe of Judah, the Jews, as those people from whom the Messiah would be born. From among the Jews he selected one family, the house of David, as the ancestors of the Messiah. God's final preparation is the beautiful story of how he brought together two of David's descendants: Joseph to be the foster father of Jesus, and Mary to be his virgin mother.

We usually take a lot of time in selecting a Christmas gift for someone we love, and we spare no expense. God's Christmas preparations were done just that way out of love for us.

DECEMBER 17th (II)

God who is big can afford to think small. From among all the possible nations in the world, he chose Judah as the ancestral homeland of his Son.

Judah enjoyed a brief golden era during the reigns of David and Solomon, but by the time Jesus was born it was nothing more than an insignificant outpost of the Roman empire. For a Roman soldier or statesman to be sent there was considered either punishment or humiliation.

And yet the bold prophecy of the Book of Genesis was verified. It was true that the scepter would never depart from Judah in the sense that the offspring of David, the king of Judah, was Jesus, the King of the universe. The tribe of Judah and the house of David were exalted far above the expectations of any prophet of the Old Testament.

The scriptures which are read at Mass on these final days of Advent show us that God chooses the weak to make them strong, that he selects the humble and the lowly to raise them up, and that he favors the poor of this world by granting them the riches of his mercy. Jacob's prophecy was something of a boast, but the boast was founded on God's mysterious ways.

We should never think that we are so small that we are not important in God's eyes. In fact, the more humble we are before God the more eager he will be to make within us a new home for his Son this Christmas.

DECEMBER 18th (I)

When St. Matthew told the Christmas story, he emphasized that the history of Israel was fulfilled in the coming of Jesus. To show God's direct intervention he pointed to Mary's virginal conception of Jesus. This divine event was, however, also a human one which was not without confusion, especially for Joseph.

What was Joseph to do when he discovered that Mary was pregnant and he knew that he was not the father? Did Mary inform him of her condition? Did she also intimate that her pregnancy was the result of a special grace from God? These questions were not answered by Matthew, but he was careful to include a key word in the angel's message to Joseph. The angel said, "Have no *fear* about taking Mary as your wife."

The Bible calls this kind of fear the beginning of wisdom. It is a reverential awe in the presence of the almighty power of God. Joseph's fear, his sense of awe, made him feel unworthy to be part of this divine event. He was an ordinary carpenter, a humble man of no particular means or reputation. But that is why God chose him. Imagine how thrilled Joseph was to learn that God wanted him to be part of the event which fulfilled the history of all his ancestors.

We must approach the Christmas event with awe and reverence, but also with the grateful realization that God calls us, ordinary though we are, to share in this great mystery.

DECEMBER 18th (II)

When the prophet Jeremiah proclaimed his message, Judah was in a sorry mess. The tiny nation was about to collapse before the mighty empire of Babylon. Jeremiah blamed the evils which had befallen the people on their kings who were like shepherds who had misled and scattered the flock. Bleak though the situation was, Jeremiah proclaimed the promise of the Lord that he would raise up a righteous king, a descendant of David.

Jeremiah's prophecy has that optimistic view of the future which characterizes our Advent liturgy. He promised that good days were coming. Even though the good days have come for us with the birth of Jesus, we look forward to even better times through our celebration of Christmas.

Advent articulates with the human experience of expectation. Advent was not invented by the Church to arouse certain sentiments within us. Advent came to be because the Church understood those instincts which God has placed within the human heart and which direct us to the events of our salvation.

Advent is the conviction that something better is around the corner. It is a hope that we will find a lost feeling of love and regain the joy of happier days.

These human sentiments are not divorced from the faith of Advent. Jeremiah's prophecy means that we have every reason to be optimistic. We must keep looking around the corner because Christ, the Good Shepherd, though present, is yet to come to us in all his glory.

DECEMBER 19th (I)

When Israel was delivered into the power of the Philistines because of her sins, God raised up Samson as a savior. An angel announced to Manoah's wife that she would conceive and bear a son. Because she had been barren, the birth of Samson was a sign that she had not conceived in the ordinary course of events, that God had intervened in a special way.

An angel appeared to Zechariah and said to him, "Your wife Elizabeth shall bear a son whom you shall name John." At the time Zechariah and Elizabeth were far beyond the age when people beget children. In this instance too there was a sign that God had intervened in a special way.

God is always at work. There is no time when he nods in sleep as might a captain who allows his airplane to fly on automatic pilot. Without God's constant action the entire universe would dissolve into nothing.

And yet there are occasions when God wants us to realize that he is acting in an extraordinary fashion for our benefit. Christmas is surely one of those occasions. In fact, both events recorded in today's reading were but a preparation for the coming of Christ into our world. The parents of Samson and the parents of the Baptist gave praise and thanks to God for the birth of their sons. How great indeed should be our response to God for the birth of his Son as our Savior!

DECEMBER 19th (II)

The story of Samson and his prodigious strength is familiar. When the Israelites were overcome by the Philistines, God raised up Samson as their savior. To show that he was an instrument of God, he was conceived by a woman who was barren. What most people remember is that he lost his power when Delilah duped him and cut off his hair. Though blinded by the hatred of the Philistines, he was able to pull down the temple of Dagon, the Philistine god, upon himself and his enemies.

One might wonder what Samson has to do with our preparations for Christmas. By contrast he helps us to appreciate the greatness of Jesus as our Savior.

Jesus is more than an instrument of God. He is divine himself. To show his unique identity, he was born of a woman who had remained a virgin in his conception. He derived his power, not from his hair, but directly from his heavenly Father.

Jesus' clear vision led him to the cross and his sacrificial offering. The cross was not a defeat. It was a great victory over the twin enemies of the human race: sin and death. His death was not a revenge upon his enemies. Rather it was while we were still sinners that Jesus died for us (cf. Romans 5:8).

Throughout history God raised up judges, prophets, and kings to help his people. In the fullness of time he showed the fullness of his love by sending us his Son.

DECEMBER 20th (I)

Catholic piety has rightly showered Mary with beautiful art and sublime poetry. A favorite scene of the masters is that of the Annunciation. Nothing short of the masterful is suitable for the Mother of God.

Some theologians, such as Pope St. Leo the Great, have emphasized a truth which art cannot depict, that Mary conceived Jesus, not only in her body, but also in her soul. This is a poetic way of saying that there was more between Jesus and Mary than a physical relationship. Jesus took from Mary his human nature, but she received from him a complete dedication to his Father's will.

Mary responded to God's message by saying, "May it be done to me according to your word." She accepted God's plan even though she could not fully understand it because she was open to the same Holy Spirit who would guide and direct Jesus throughout his life on this earth. Her heart was filled with the spirit of Jesus even before her womb was filled with the presence of Jesus.

Christmas will have real meaning for us in the degree that we become like Mary. In order for Christ to come alive within us in a renewed birth, we need to share in her dedication to God's will, even in matters we cannot fully understand. In our offering of the Lord's prayer during the eucharist we have the opportunity to follow the example of Mary as we say, "Thy will be done."

DECEMBER 20th (II)

In that sublime moment described in today's gospel the eternal Son of God became human in the womb of Mary. Precisely how God accomplished this conception without a human father we do not know, but we can rightly say that Mary gave to Jesus his heredity. Like mother, like son applied to Mary and Jesus. As Jesus was growing up, people noticed the physical resemblance. He reminded them of Mary.

God the Father willed that Jesus would have a physical resemblance to Mary, but it was his wish that Mary bear a spiritual resemblance to Jesus. To Mary, as well as to us, the words of St. Paul are applicable: "Those whom God foreknew he predestined to share the image of his Son, that the Son might be the firstborn of many brothers and sisters" (Romans 8:29).

To share the image of the Son is not only to be like Jesus but to act like him. The mother of Jesus was his first and chief disciple. She is the example of what every Christian should be.

Devotion to Mary was brought to a sharp and brilliant focus by the Second Vatican Council in its Dogmatic Constitution on the Church (#53). The Council declared: "Mary is the pre-eminent and altogether singular member of the Church, and she is the Church's model and excellent exemplar in faith and love." How should we relate to Jesus? That is the question Mary answers.

DECEMBER 21st (I)

When someone appears to be grumpy or moody these days, we ask them, "What's the matter with you? Don't you have the Christmas spirit?" Even though we cannot define the Christmas spirit, we know it means putting aside selfishness and offering cheerful help to others.

In today's gospel we see a beautiful example of the full meaning of the Christmas spirit from no less than Mary herself. When she heard that her elderly relative Elizabeth had conceived, Mary wasted no time. She left immediately for Elizabeth's house. It was a journey of perhaps seventy miles which, we presume, Mary made on foot, probably traveling with some other women from Nazareth. One can imagine that Joseph was worried about her making the trip, and perhaps even protested, but Mary was eager to be of help.

At this time Mary had already conceived Jesus. When Elizabeth saw Mary, she was given the grace to perceive how different she was from her companions who had come from Nazareth. Elizabeth was given the grace to recognize Mary as the most favored of all women because of the child she was to bear. Mary had come to offer her services, and what she accomplished was to bring Christ himself to Elizabeth and to the child in her womb.

We ourselves appear as ordinary as the women who accompanied Mary, but the truth is that our unselfish love and willing service bring Christ to others. That is the Christmas spirit.

DECEMBER 21st (II)

Pope John XXIII was a jolly person who had little use for pessimists whom he dubbed "the prophets of doom." The prophet Zephaniah, however, had good reason to be a pessimist. The people of Jerusalem had fallen back into old idolatries and worshipped the sun, moon, and stars rather than the Lord, their creator.

Although Zephaniah warned about a day of doom, his faith in God would not allow him to remain negative. He promised that the Lord in his mercy would spare a holy remnant. Today's reading is the prophet's optimistic conclusion in which he encourages the faithful to be joyful because the Lord, their God, a mighty Savior, is in their midst.

Elizabeth was like a prophet of joyful hope, not doom. Her words form part of a favorite prayer in honor of Mary: "Blessed are you among women and blessed is the fruit of your womb." Elizabeth was given the grace to recognize that the Lord, though yet unborn, had come to her through Mary, and she declared that her baby's stirring within her was his joyful response to the presence of Jesus.

Faith moves us to believe that Jesus came into this world through Mary, and that he continues to live both among us and within us. Some people could give a long list of woes which are a cause for pessimism, but the Lord's presence among us and within us is a cause for that joyful attitude which we call the Christmas spirit.

DECEMBER 21st (III)

Today's first reading is one of many love poems which make up a book in the Bible known as the Song of Songs. Since this book does not even mention God, some people wonder what it is doing among the inspired works of sacred scripture.

The reality of Christmas should help to put this book into perspective. We recognize that Jesus, born of Mary, is both human and divine. We call the truth that God took flesh and lived among us the incarnation.

The Second Vatican Council has given us this beautiful teaching in its Constitution on the Church in the Modern World (#22): "By his incarnation the Son of God has united himself in some fashion with every human person. He worked with human hands, thought with a human mind, acted by human choice, and loved with a human heart. He showed us the way, and if we follow it, life and death are made holy and take on a new meaning."

Everything that God created is good and holy, but the incarnation gives a special sacredness to all things human. In the kind of love which is celebrated in the Song of Songs, God's great love and fidelity are not merely represented. His love and fidelity are contained in human love.

At Christmas we look to the crib to see God in the human flesh of a baby. From that scene we must look up to find God all around us.

"The Church considers the Christmas season,
which celebrates the birth of our Lord
and his early manifestations, second only
to the annual celebration of the Easter mystery"
(Norms for the Liturgical Year and Calendar, 32).

DECEMBER 22nd (I)

The song of Mary in today's gospel, known by its Latin name, the "Magnificat," is not her original composition. It bears a strong resemblance to the song of Samuel's mother, Hannah, which is used in today's liturgy as a response to the first reading. The Magnificat also reflects a number of other Old Testament passages.

One beauty of the Magnificat is that it both expresses the sentiments of Mary and reflects a long tradition of solid piety in the Old Testament. When Elizabeth praised Mary as the most favored of all women, Mary responded according to that tradition. In effect she said to Elizabeth, "Do not give the credit to me. Rather join me in proclaiming the greatness of the Lord; together we can find joy in God our Savior."

We share in the favor which was granted to Mary by God. She was indeed the most blessed of women because of the fruit of her womb. But we are most blessed, too, because her child who is God's divine Son has become our Savior.

The Magnificat is held in such high esteem by the Church that it is part of her evening prayer every day of the year. That fact is an invitation to us to offer this beautiful prayer of solid piety, whether we pray the Liturgy of the Hours or not. Mary wants us to join her in saying, "My being proclaims the greatness of the Lord and my spirit finds joy in God my Savior."

DECEMBER 22nd (II)

The spirit of Christmas is one of generosity. This spirit flows from God himself and is exemplified in today's liturgical readings.

Hannah had been barren. She prayed for a son and made a vow that she would offer him to the service of the Lord. Shortly after his birth, Hannah and her husband brought their son, Samuel, to the temple and left him there to grow up under the priest Eli.

At a time when Mary had apparently become a widow she allowed her only child to begin his public ministry on our behalf. Her action was unselfish and filled with zeal for God's work of salvation.

Hannah's son, Samuel, trained by the priest Eli, became a great prophet who anointed Saul as Israel's first king and who later anointed David as its greatest king. Mary's son, Jesus, both prophet and king, was the priest who offered the sacrifice of the cross for our salvation.

Both women reflect the goodness of God. We can only imagine how precious Samuel was to Hannah and Jesus was to Mary. For them to give up their sons was unselfish and courageous. But we cannot even begin to comprehend the love of God the Father for his Son. And yet the Father so loved us that he gave us his only Son as our Savior.

Christmas is incomplete without giving. But the best gift is not an object; it is the love which we give to God and his people.

DECEMBER 23rd (I)

Parents have many reasons for choosing the name of their child. In the case of the Baptist, God himself, and not the parents, determined his name as part of the revelation of the meaning of Christmas. The name, "John," suggests an important truth about the coming of the Lord into our world. In its full Hebrew form it can be translated as "The Lord is gracious," or "The Lord shows favor." The birth of Jesus came about because God in his graciousness wanted to show us his favor.

The word "favor" often refers to a trivial matter, but it really means any response which is freely given. It is not a favor to an employee that the boss pays him or her a day's wage for a day's work; that is due in justice. But it is a favor that God sends his Son as our Savior.

The word used by the angel when he announced to Mary that she would be the Mother of God's Son reflects the revelation contained in the name John. The angel said, "Hail, full of grace." This greeting meant that Mary was God's most highly favored daughter; she was filled with his graciousness. She did nothing to merit her vocation as the mother of Jesus. It was all God's doing.

We have done nothing to merit God's favor. Christmas is his gift to us. He is so gracious that he gave us the greatest gift possible, his own Son.

DECEMBER 23rd (II)

When the Jews returned to the promised land after their exile in Babylon, they struggled in poverty amid the riches of the land's occupants. They complained to God that only the evildoers prospered. Despite their personal infidelities, they demanded to know when God would fulfill his promises of blessings.

Malachi replied as best he could. Prophet though he was, he did not clearly envision the coming of Christ as our Savior. If he had, he could have given a much brighter picture of the future to the poor.

In our own day we may at times wonder about the prosperity of people who seem to have no regard for God or his laws. We must then remember the revelation which is ours. No one is excluded from the love of Christ. The rich and powerful are included, as witness the welcome given to the Magi. And yet the poor, the simple, and the humble do receive special favor. The first to come to the crib were the shepherds, who represented plain, ordinary people, who depended on God and not their wealth.

Mary in her "Magnificat" praised God because "he has scattered the proud in their conceit; he has cast down the mighty from their thrones, and has lifted up the lowly."

We will receive the blessings of Christmas to the degree that we are humble before the Lord, and that we depend, not on the wealth of this world, but on the riches of God's mercy.

DECEMBER 24th (I)

Tomorrow is Christmas. It is a day which fulfills the promises God made through his prophets to satisfy the yearnings of people for centuries from the time of Abraham.

Zechariah's canticle is a hymn of praise and thanks to God for his faithfulness. In it the coming of the Lord is likened to the dawn, the light which comes into a darkened world.

Christmas is a feast of light. It occurs when we have concluded the shortest day of the year and light begins to increase. At midnight Mass, in the depth of darkness, we hear the encouraging words of Isaiah: "The people who walked in darkness have seen a great light; upon those who dwelt in the land of gloom a light has shone."

To walk in darkness is to stumble and fall, but to walk in the light is to be secure and sure on the right path. We know that as a pilgrim people we are on the right way home because we have Christ our Light to guide us.

Zechariah's canticle, which is known by its Latin name, "The Benedictus," is part of the Church's morning prayer. Whether we pray the Liturgy of the Hours or not, we ought to realize that every morning is like Christmas, that the dawn is a symbol of the coming of Christ. Not only on Christmas, but every day of our lives, we ought to give thanks and praise to God for the gift of his Son.

DECEMBER 24th (II)

King David wanted to build a temple, a house for the Lord to express his gratitude for all the Lord had done for him. The prophet Nathan thought it was a great idea until the Lord told him that he did not need nor want a house to live in. Rather he would establish a house for David, meaning a dynasty and kingdom, that would endure forever.

This promise became the basis of Jewish expectation of a kingly Messiah, the Son of David. We are Christians today because God fulfilled this promise.

At midnight Mass the gospel tells us that Joseph took Mary from the town of Nazareth to David's town of Bethlehem. There Jesus was born and the angel proclaimed: "This day in David's city a Savior has been born to you, the Messiah and Lord."

From the time of Nathan's promise God narrowed the focus of his light until it illumined David's city of Bethlehem. From that time the light shining from the crib of Bethlehem has broadened to include the whole world. That light shines on us tomorrow to brighten our spirits and guide us on our way. We will relive some of the most tender scenes and warmest emotions of our religion as once again we look upon an infant who is more than a descendant of David. A divine light reveals to us that he is the Son of God.

"The Church includes in the annual cycle days devoted to the memory of the martyrs and the other saints. Raised up to perfection by the manifold grace of God, and already in possession of eternal salvation, they sing God's perfect praise in heaven and offer prayers for us. By celebrating the passage of these saints from earth to heaven the Church proclaims the paschal mystery as achieved in the saints who have suffered and been glorified with Christ. She proposes them to the faithful as examples who draw all to the Father through Christ, and through their merits she pleads for God's favors."

(*Constitution on the Sacred Liturgy*, 104)

Part Three

SAINTS' DAYS
DURING ADVENT

NOVEMBER 30
FEAST OF SAINT ANDREW, APOSTLE

St. Andrew had to live under the shadow of his more famous and, we may presume, older brother, Peter. Anyone who has an older brother or sister knows how Andrew felt. There were times when it seemed that he had no identity of his own. He was Peter's brother. Even when the two boys were growing up, it is not unlikely that the parents would say to Andrew, "Why can't you be like your big brother?"

We can be quite certain that Andrew came to accept his role of being the younger brother of a famous person. But that person was not Peter. It was Jesus.

It pleased God to make Jesus the firstborn of many brothers and sisters. Those whom God foreknew he predestined to share the image of his Son (Romans 8:29). Such was God's plan for St. Andrew, a calling more fundamental than his vocation to be a fisher of men. It is our calling, too.

God our Father never berates us by saying "Why can't you be like your older brother?" but he does invite us to become like his beloved Son as part of his family. We are brothers and sisters of Jesus because God is our Father.

Advent is a time to study Jesus in the gospels. It is a time for us to grow in becoming more like him through the power of the eucharist. Advent is a time for watching big brother.

DECEMBER 3
MEMORIAL OF SAINT FRANCIS XAVIER

Francis Xavier was born in Spain in 1506. When he was twenty-four he met St. Ignatius Loyola and became one of the first Jesuits. He was ordained a priest in 1537 and a few years later was sent as a missionary to the Far East where he preached the gospel in India, Sri Lanka, and Japan. He died at the age of forty-six as he was about to enter China. So great was his zeal that he has been named patron of the missions.

Francis Xavier was a faithful disciple of Jesus whom God the Father sent into our world "to bring glad tidings to the poor, to proclaim liberty to captives, recovery of sight to the blind, and release to prisoners" (Luke 4:18). Christ was born again in Francis and through him lived his life of love.

This Christmas Christ wants to be born again in us. He may be calling some to bring him to the foreign missions, but whatever our state in life, Jesus invites us to allow him to continue, through us, his life of love.

He wants to use our voices to give praise to his heavenly Father. He wants to use our hands to nurse the sick and to feed the hungry. He wants to use our hearts to show his affection for the poor, the underprivileged, and the outcasts of our society.

Will Christ this Christmas again find no room, or will we with warmth and courage welcome him into our lives?

DECEMBER 6
OPTIONAL MEMORIAL OF SAINT NICHOLAS

The facts we know about St. Nicholas are few; he existed, he was a bishop in Asia Minor, and he had a Greek name which he shares with five popes. The first part of his name is the Greek word for victory, *nike*, and the second part is the Greek word for people, *laos*, from which we have derived our word, laity, to designate those who have been baptized. His name literally means "the victory of the people."

Legends about the generous gift-giving of St. Nicholas have abounded through the Dutch version of his name, Santa Claus. That name recalls some of the most delightful experiences of childhood, and suggests jolliness and good-natured generosity. Santa Claus represents unselfishness. He is the gift giver who never receives a gift himself.

Behind all these legends is the human yearning for the fulfillment of the proclamation by Jesus: "The reign of God is at hand." God's reign is a kingdom of justice, of love, and of peace.

People of faith should proclaim the reality of God's kingdom by words and by actions. Each of us should be a "Nicholas" and not a "Scrooge." As the baptized people of God we should manifest the victory of Christ over sin and selfishness and over bleakness and pessimism. We are called to be a people of justice, love, and peace.

DECEMBER 7
MEMORIAL OF SAINT AMBROSE

Ambrose was sent to Milan to be its Roman governor and ended by becoming its bishop. We honor him on December 7th because on this day in the year 374 he was ordained bishop. He feast day is now inescapably linked with the memory of the bombing of Pearl Harbor and the entry of the United States into the Second World War.

There is an irony in this connection since Ambrose turned away from political and military power to embrace Christ and his Church. His master was no longer the emperor but the Prince of Peace.

Although Ambrose was a fiery man who engaged in disputes with the powerful figures of his day, his main concern was to win people to Christ, and he claimed the great Augustine as his convert. Although he had studied the Latin classics and even modeled some of his sermons on the oratory of Cicero, his chief dedication was to the sacred scriptures.

His feast day is followed quite appropriately by that of the Immaculate Conception. Ambrose wrote extensively on the importance of Mary in God's plan of salvation.

Who knows what Ambrose would have been without Christ? Actually he is only one of many brilliant and capable people whose lives were transformed by Christ and who dedicated themselves to his service rather than pursue their own interests. Ambrose should inspire all of us to renew our dedication to Christ and to deepen a resolve to follow him alone.

DECEMBER 8
SOLEMNITY OF THE IMMACULATE CONCEPTION

Mary was conceived without sin. That immaculate conception prepared her for the moment described in the gospel today when through the power of the Holy Spirit Jesus was conceived in her womb.

It is impossible for us to celebrate Christmas without thinking of Mary. Jesus was conceived without a human father, but not even Jesus came into this world without a human mother. Because God alone is Father to Jesus, Mary takes on a more prominent role than would ordinarily be true of a mother. Mary is inseparable from Jesus.

During the Christmas season we will see many cards and pictures depicting a lovely young mother holding an infant. Nothing appears unusual to an unbeliever except perhaps the fact that the scene is not a modern one. This is the way it should be. The first reality to strike us about Christmas should be the truth that at a certain time in history a human mother gave birth to a human child. Jesus is human like us in all things but sin, and Mary is the source of his humanity.

Anyone who stops short with accepting the humanity of Jesus has not been open to God's grace and the light of revelation. Jesus is truly divine as well as human. The doctrine of the Church that Mary is the mother of God has its roots in the Church's understanding of who Jesus is.

The matter came to a focus when Bishop Nestorius of Constantinople began teaching that Jesus not only has two natures, which is Catholic doctrine, but that these natures are so distinct that Jesus is actually two persons, which is an heretical opinion. A crisis broke out when Nestorius maintained that Mary was the mother of the human person of

Christ but not of the divine person, the Son of God. Nestorius denied to Mary the title, "Mother of God."

The Council of Ephesus in the year 431 ruled definitively against Nestorius. This Council solemnly declared that Mary is indeed the Mother of God since there is only one person in Jesus, not two, and that person is divine, the Son of God.

Following this declaration, feasts in honor of Mary began to multiply and spread. It is fitting that the title "Mother of God" should have been the source from which Marian devotion in the Church developed.

Catholic doctrine never separates Mary from her divine Son. It is a serious error when any devotion suggests that Mary is equal to Jesus, or that she is more compassionate than he, or that we may concentrate on her alone. It is also very sad that some who are not of the Catholic faith fail to understand and appreciate the place of Mary in God's plan for the incarnation of his Son.

God the Father preserved Mary free from sin, even from the moment of her conception, in preparation for that moment when his Son became her Son.

DECEMBER 12
OUR LADY OF GUADALUPE

Some people become a little upset when they see a Christmas card which represents Mary as having blond hair and blue eyes. After all, God the Creator formed and fashioned a Semitic maiden from the tribe of Judah, of the house and family of David, to be the human mother of his divine Son.

It seems right to depict Mary as a lovely young girl of olive smooth complexion, her raven hair parted in the middle and falling over her shoulders, her dark eyes dancing with the joy of the new life that developed within her, the significance of which even she could not comprehend.

Actually the objection to the blond version (some might say the "Hollywood" version) of Mary is a form of fundamentalism. The fact is that Mary was the Jewish mother of the messianic son of David, but the truth goes beyond even that wondrous reality. Mary is the mother of God. The divine identity of her Son moved her to be more than his mother; she became his first and chief disciple.

Mary is the model and exemplar for all those who respond to the Messiah as his faithful disciples, those people who become united with Christ in his mystical body, the Church. Mary, like the Church, is Jewish in origin, but like the Church she is universal in essence.

The Church does not turn a foreign-looking face to any nation or people. The Church is not Italian or Irish any more than it is Iranian or Iraqui. It is universal. For that reason it is right for people to see Mary as a reflection of themselves.

Mary is the Indian-looking Lady of Guadalupe and she is the French-looking Lady of the Miraculous Medal. She is as much Our Lady, Queen of Saigon as she is Our Lady, Queen of Angels.

Sometimes Christians who are not of the Catholic faith wonder why we emphasize the place of Mary. One reason is the different understanding of, to use a technical word, ecclesiology, the theology of the Church. As Catholics we adhere to the truth that it has pleased God to save us and to make us holy by forming us into a single people, a people who worship him in truth and who serve him in holiness. We believe that these people are the Church of which Mary is the model and exemplar.

We never celebrate Mass, that distinctive act which identifies us as Catholics, without an invocation of Mary, the Mother of God. She is named in every eucharistic prayer because the eucharist is the sacrament of the unity of the Church of which Mary is the personification.

During the season of Advent as we prepare to celebrate the birth of our Savior we observe two important feasts of Mary, the Immaculate Conception on December 8th (wherein she is depicted as she is seen on the miraculous medal) and Our Lady of Guadalupe on December 12th (wherein she is depicted as she was seen on the cloak of Juan Diego). These images are not contradictory. Together they help us to realize the essentially Catholic aspect of our faith.

DECEMBER 13
MEMORIAL OF SAINT LUCY

Liturgical tradition has a great affection for four young girls.
They are Agatha, Agnes, Cecilia and Lucy. They were all virgins
and martyrs, and each has her feast day during the year.*

St. Lucy was executed for her faith in Sicily around the year
304. Nothing more is known about her with certainty, but the
lack of facts has not daunted devotion to her. The liturgy is
more concerned with truth than with facts, and the beautiful
truth is that a humble young girl, considered weak and lowly by
her tormentors, found a strength in Christ which was greater
than that which even an emperor could muster against her.

Jesus was born poor amid humble surroundings to show
his favor to the needy of this world. Despite his apparent lack of
military and monetary resources which an emperor would
have considered indispensable, Jesus came to strengthen the
weak, to exalt the humble, and to lift up the lowly.

The name Lucy is from the Latin word for light. By her life
and martyrdom, St. Lucy enlightens us about the real values of
life. She also helps us to see that we can persevere in
faithfulness to God despite obstacles and difficulties. There is a
great strength to be gained from depending on Christ. That
strength is ours, as it was for Lucy, through prayer and
especially through the sacrament of the body and the blood of
Christ.

_____

* Agatha on Feb. 5, Agnes on Jan. 21, and Cecilia on Nov. 22.

DECEMBER 14
MEMORIAL OF SAINT JOHN OF THE CROSS

St. John of the Cross was a Carmelite priest who led a life dedicated to prayer and mortification. His liturgical memorial always falls within the season of Advent. This is not so because there is any special relationship of this saint to Advent but because he died on this day in the year 1591. The liturgy, as far as possible, honors a saint on the day of death which is considered the day of birth into everlasting life.

And yet John of the Cross may well remind us of an important Advent figure, John the Baptist. The similarity goes beyond their names.

Both men centered their entire lives on the person of Christ. Both were austere and both considered no effort too great in order to embrace Christ, no sacrifice too difficult to overcome any obstacle to grow in Christ. John the Baptist went off to the desert to fast and pray, and John of the Cross retired to his cell for the same purpose.

During these busy days of Advent which can be filled with many distractions as we get ready for Christmas, these two saints remind us that we must focus on the person of Christ. It is his birthday for which we are preparing. They also show us that we really ought to devote some quiet time to prayer and reflection as important ways of preparing to celebrate the real meaning of Christmas.

"The Lenten season has a
twofold character: 1) it recalls baptism or
prepares for it; 2) it stresses a penitential
spirit. By these means especially,
Lent readies the faithful for
celebrating the paschal mystery after
a period of closer attention to the
Word of God, and more ardent prayer."

(Constitution on the Sacred Liturgy, 109)

Part Four

THE WEEKDAYS
OF LENT

ASH WEDNESDAY (I)

The ashes in today's ceremony are produced by burning the branches left from last year's Palm Sunday. The palms which had been the symbol of the triumphant kingship of Christ have been transformed into ashes which are the sign of humility, even of death.

The Christian life is the other way around. Ashes are turned into palm branches. In the paschal mystery sorrow is changed into joy, humiliation is lifted up to glory, and death is overcome by life.

For us repentance is the first half of the paschal mystery. We must be honest about our sins and our weaknesses and resolve with God's grace to overcome them. We begin Lent today, however, not on a note of despair or even discouragement. Rather our hearts should be filled with hope because our eyes should be lifted up to God who created the paschal mystery.

The paschal mystery is a favorite idea of God. He applied it to the Israelites when he led them from slavery to freedom in the exodus. He applied it to Jesus when he raised him from death to the glory of the resurrection. And he wishes to apply it to us during Lent by transforming our repentance into the fullness of his life and love.

Some people do not like Lent, but God loves it because it delights him to continue the paschal mystery. It will please him to transform the ashes of our Lenten penance into the joyful triumph of Easter Sunday.

ASH WEDNESDAY (II)

The Church applies to Ash Wednesday, the beginning of Lent, the words of St. Paul "Now is the acceptable time. Now is the day of salvation."

Older Catholics remark that Lent isn't what it used to be. There are only two days of fasting, today, Ash Wednesday, and Good Friday. All Fridays of Lent are days of abstinence. Pretty simple.

One reason for this simplicity in external observances is that, although we are a community as the people of the Church, we are also individuals. Each of us has specific needs which cannot be met by uniform practices.

Each one of us must take the responsibility to determine what our greatest need is. Lent is a grace to look at ourselves honestly. A guide for this examination of conscience is found in the penitential rite at Mass. First is the spirit of honesty before God: we admit that we have sinned through our own fault. Secondly, this prayer tells us that we must consider our failings and weaknesses in our thoughts and in our words, in what we have done and in what we have failed to do. Thirdly, it lifts our spirits in the realization that we have the help of the prayers of Mary, the angels and saints, and all our fellow Catholics who are our brothers and sisters.

Lent is not next month or next week, or tomorrow. Lent is today. Now is the acceptable time for repentance and renewal.

THURSDAY AFTER ASH WEDNESDAY (I)

Some time ago a well-known evangelist announced that God had revealed to him that unless he received several million dollars in gifts, he would die. Without judging the man personally, it must be observed that he had it backwards. Jesus says that we must die in order to obtain the riches of everlasting life.

It is not surprising that the evangelist was mistaken. Jesus' doctrine is hard to understand and even harder to accept. He tells us to deny ourselves, to take up our cross each day, and to follow in his steps. Only the one who loses his life will save it.

Lent is a time for us to reflect on whether we have accepted the Christian paradox or whether we are living life backwards. Do we seek leisure in place of work? Do we want to be first rather than last? Are we quick to speak but slow to listen? Do we always insist on our own way? Do we look for comfort in prayer rather than making an offering of ourselves with Christ crucified in the sacrifice of the Mass?

Are we looking for a resurrection without the cross?

THURSDAY AFTER ASH WEDNESDAY (II)

Moses issued a summons to his people to be faithful to God's commandments. That is the way to love God. Jesus says, "Whoever wishes to be my follower must deny his very self, take up his cross each day, and follow in my steps." That is the way to love God.

St. Vincent de Paul lived by an exhortation which he proclaimed to his followers: "Let us love God, let us love God, but let it be at the expense of our arms and in the sweat of our brows." He explained that affection for God in prayer, though good and desirable in itself, is questionable when it is not translated into practical love.

St. Vincent lamented the fact that some people can speak like angels about their experiences in prayer but are nowhere to be found when it comes to working for God, to suffering, to taking care of the poor, or to instructing children in the faith. He said, "The Church is compared with a great harvest which demands laborers, but what is needed is laborers who labor."

Words are not love; actions are. During the penitential rite of the Mass we express sorrow, not only for what we have done, but also for what we have failed to do. To form good Lenten resolutions we need to reflect on what we leave undone. The answer leads us to love God at the expense of our arms and in the sweat of our brows.

FRIDAY AFTER ASH WEDNESDAY (I)

When the people returned from exile in Babylon to the promised land, they began to complain about their lack of prosperity. They protested that the Lord seemed absent from their lives even though they were fasting and mortifying themselves.

What was the problem? They were quite precise about following the rules, but they had lost a vision of the meaning of mortification. They were like those who objected to Jesus that his disciples were not fasting in the manner of the Pharisees.

Any form of mortification is not an end in itself. The word implies a dying to oneself, a putting to death of selfishness. Its purpose is to turn our eyes and our attention away from ourselves toward God and his people. We have to take care of ourselves, but the spirit of fasting calls us to keep that care to a minimum so that we may respond to those who are in need all around us. We limit attention to ourselves so that we may focus in love on others.

The reading from Isaiah presents us with a program for Lent. God through his prophet says to us: "This is the fasting I wish: sharing your bread with the hungry, sheltering the oppressed and the homeless, clothing the naked when you see them, and not turning your back on your own."

When we help those in need, the Lord says "Here I am. You have found me."

FRIDAY AFTER ASH WEDNESDAY (II)

Most people do not like fasting. It is difficult and does not have any observable results. Most people do not even like dieting despite its observable results. And so it is consoling to hear the response which Jesus gave to those who objected that his disciples were not fasting. He said, "How can the wedding guests go in mourning so long as the groom is with them?" Christ, the groom is surely with us and so we do not have to worry about fasting.

But is Christ with us in all our thoughts, all our words, and all our actions?

Christ is not in our thoughts when we harbor resentment against people or make rash judgments about them. We must fast from such thoughts.

Christ is not in our words when we repeat gossip, when we spread rumors, and when we blacken the good name of others. We must fast from such words.

Christ is not in our actions when we hurt people's feelings by ignoring them, or when we indulge in laziness and act only for our own benefit. We must fast from such actions.

We need to remember the conclusion of today's gospel. Jesus said, "When the groom is taken away, then they will fast." In any of our thoughts, words, or actions do we drive Christ away?

SATURDAY AFTER ASH WEDNESDAY (I)

I think we have all heard someone say, "I don't want to go to the doctor; he may find something wrong with me." We may have said that ourselves. The temptation is to let things go and hope that whatever is wrong will clear up by itself. The problem is that some people let something go so long that nothing can be done. They end up with incurable cancer.

Lent is a time for a spiritual checkup with Christ, our divine physician. We need to set aside time to examine our lives before him. If there is something wrong, we should talk to him about it in prayer. If we are harboring some sin, it is foolish to let it grow like an invisible cancer. We need to tell Christ about that in the sacrament of penance.

Even venial sins are significant. Although it is contrary to Catholic teaching to think that a number of venial sins can add up to a mortal sin, we should not ignore them. Love for God should move us to want to exclude even venial sins from our lives.

It would be a mistake to allow some spiritual problem to continue beyond Easter. Lent is the grace-filled opportunity for action. We should not want to keep anything from Christ, nor should we try to deceive ourselves in our minds or the priest in confession. Now is the time for perfect honesty with the right person, Christ, our divine physician.

SATURDAY AFTER ASH WEDNESDAY (II)

Most people cherish their names and want them to be respected. Today we must accept an additional name, the name of sinner. Jesus said in the gospel, "I have not come to invite the self-righteous to a change of heart, but sinners."

When you think about it, it is not so bad being named a sinner. In a sense it is better than not being able to be a sinner. You will never sit upon a sinful rock, or watch a sinful bird in flight, or play with a sinful dog. In this world only we human beings can be sinners. The ability to sin indicates a great trust from God, and reveals our potential to become more than we are.

A rock, solid though it is, cannot possess the solid foundation of faith. We can. A bird can fly in the sky, but it cannot fly to heaven. We can. A dog is man's best friend, but he cannot be God's friend the way we can.

If we did not have the potential to become more than we are now, we would not be capable of sin, for sin is the rejection of our potential. Looking at it another way, Jesus speaks of sin in terms of being sick. No one could be called sick if there were not a state called health.

In admitting our sinfulness we acknowledge our potential for greatness. When Jesus says that he calls sinners, we can joyfully respond: "Here I am. You have called *me*."

MONDAY OF THE FIRST WEEK OF LENT (I)

Some people have an image in their minds of what a saint looks like. He is thin, if not emaciated. He kneels for long hours in the back of a darkened church, his eyes closed, his face buried in his hands, his brow wrinkled by intense concentration. He seems oblivious of his surroundings as he communes with God present within his being. He goes through life as one lifted above mere mortals and their foibles.

We need personal prayer, but today's readings are a clear call to action. Jesus in the gospel moves us, when we have completed our prayer, to take our hands away from our faces and to open our eyes to see those who are in need. He urges us to rise from our knees and to go to feed the hungry, to welcome the stranger, to clothe the naked, to comfort the sick, and to visit those in prison.

Jesus gives the reason for his exhortation. We find him not only in prayer but also in those who are in need, even those who might be considered the least of his brothers and sisters.

It is not ours to judge who is saintly. That judgment is left to God who guides the Church in its process of canonization. But we do have a clear teaching in the gospel today to guide us in daily living. Whatever else may be necessary for holiness, true sanctity cannot be achieved while ignoring Christ in his people.

MONDAY OF THE FIRST WEEK OF LENT (II)

Belief in the real presence of Christ in the Blessed Sacrament is indispensable to our Catholic faith. You simply cannot be a Catholic without it. But this belief is incomplete without a belief in his real presence in people.

We must not water down the teaching of Jesus in the gospel: "Whatever you do, even to the least of my brothers and sisters, you do to me."

For many people believing that Christ is really present in the Blessed Sacrament is easier than believing that Christ is really present in people. This is what I mean. Christ in the Blessed Sacrament does not annoy us. He does not get on our nerves. He does not put demands upon us. But people do.

Christ in the Blessed Sacrament does not yell at us, or bug us about not smoking, and he never insists on watching his program on TV when we want to see something else. But people do.

Christ in the Blessed Sacrament does not fail to thank us for favors. He does not need a bath. He does not ask us for money so that he can get something to eat when we really suspect that he is going to spend the money on booze. But people do.

We cannot pick and choose. We believe that Christ is present in the Blessed Sacrament and we must act accordingly. We must believe that Christ is present in people and act accordingly, too.

TUESDAY OF THE FIRST WEEK OF LENT (I)

Three of the most beautiful words in our language are, "I love you." They reach a high point in the relationship which we call marriage. Human relationships, however, are not always smooth. There are ups and downs. Often when there are downs, one of the persons must say, "I am sorry." And then comes one of the greatest tests of love. Can the other person say and really mean, "I forgive you"?

The prayer taught us by Jesus today is uplifting. It reflects our most profound relationship with God as our Father. And yet within this bright, optimistic prayer there is a recognition that our relationship with God sometimes goes down. And so we are taught to say, "Forgive our trespasses."

What is God's response? It is a word of forgiveness. It is a powerful word which wipes out our guilt. Isaiah declares that God's word achieves the end for which he sends it, like the rain which waters the earth. The context of this passage from Isaiah indicates that this word is one of forgiveness. Isaiah says, "Let the sinner turn to the Lord for mercy, to our God who is generous in forgiving."

The price of God's forgiveness indicates the height of his love. That price is the blood of Jesus, which was shed so that sins might be forgiven.

God is our loving Father. One of the greatest signs of his love is found in the three words, "I forgive you."

TUESDAY OF THE FIRST WEEK OF LENT (II)

The Church prays the "Our Father" three times a day, at morning prayer, at evening prayer, and at Mass. This practice follows the exhortation of the Didache, a treatise from the early second century.

This simple prayer is more than a sublime form of prayer which is a norm for other prayers. It indicates our relationship with God as our Father and expresses our identity as his sons and daughters.

When infants are baptized, the priest says to the participants: "These children have been reborn in baptism. They are now called children of God, for so indeed they are. They will call God their Father in the midst of the Church." Then as a climax to the ceremony all present say the "Our Father" in the name of the newly baptized children.

Adults in the catechumenate during Lent are presented with a copy of this prayer as a gift from God and his Church. Following their baptism when they take part in their first celebration of the eucharist, they will say it together with the rest of the baptized.

We say this prayer so frequently that we can become dulled to its meaning. Although we ought to attend to all the words, we should at least never lose sight of the first two words. God is truly our Father, and we are truly his children. Nothing is a greater reality for us than our relationship with God.

WEDNESDAY OF THE FIRST WEEK OF LENT (I)

Today's gospel is surprising if not shocking. We heard words from Jesus which sounded like groans of frustration.

Jesus observed that Jonah by his preaching moved the Ninevites to repentance. And Jonah was not a very virtuous man. He ran away from his mission and had to be forced by God to preach to the Ninevites by being brought close to death in the episode about the great fish. But Jonah succeeded in a way which Jesus did not. No wonder Jesus felt frustrated.

Jesus observed that Solomon was renowned for his wisdom, and the Queen of Sheba traveled a great distance to hear him. But Solomon with all his wisdom was guilty of sins so great that they helped to bring about the disintegration of God's people into two separate kingdoms. Solomon gained a hearing which Jesus did not. No wonder Jesus felt frustrated.

How does Jesus feel about us? Lent is a time for repentance through self-denial. Do we follow this teaching of Jesus or do we find that we are more influenced by the self-indulgent outlook of our culture? Lent is an invitation to grow in wisdom by devoting more time to prayer and the reading of the scriptures? Do we make opportunities for this wisdom or do we give in to the tempting availability of ubiquitous entertainment in our society?

We have no one greater than Jesus in our lives. How does he feel about us?

WEDNESDAY OF THE FIRST WEEK OF LENT (II)

Almost everyone has received in the mail one of those promotional contest forms which promises that "you too could win a million dollars, no purchase necessary." Of course the promoters hope you will make a purchase, and they make everything as easy as possible, even to supplying a postage-paid envelope.

God wanted to make repentance as easy as possible for the Ninevites. The prophet Jonah had other ideas. He hated the Ninevites and preferred to see them destroyed. But God insisted. After the episode with the great fish, Jonah realized that God was serious and so he went and preached to the Ninevites who responded with the enthusiasm of someone intent on winning a million dollars.

God has done even more for us. He has given us, not Jonah, but his Son who is as greater than Jonah as heaven is greater than a million dollars. Through the death and resurrection of his Son, God the Father has sent the Holy Spirit among us for the forgiveness of sins.

Accepting God's invitation to repentance leads us to the sacrament of penance. This sacrament is not a contest. In a contest the outcome is unknown; all depends on the luck of the draw. The outcome of our confession is as certain as God's love.

Forgiveness from God which follows our repentance is worth infinitely more than a million dollars. No purchase is necessary because no purchase is possible for God's gift of forgiveness.

THURSDAY OF THE FIRST WEEK OF LENT (I)

Sometimes we need to be cautioned not to overdo prayers of petition and to remember to give thanks and praise to God. And yet prayer of petition can and should be a beautiful expression of our relationship with God.

In the Gospel we hear Jesus allude to the response of good parents. He asks, "Would one of you hand his child a stone when he asks for bread?" Certainly the child does not expect to receive a stone. When a child asks for something from his parents, he is acknowledging two qualities about them, even though he may not be able to express those qualities in words.

First, he believes that his parents have power. A little child thinks that his parents are almighty, that they can do anything. Secondly, he believes that his parents will use their power to answer his request because they love him.

Power and love are the qualities of God which we acknowledge when we address prayers of petition to him. These prayers are an important form of worship, and the liturgy emphasizes them during the Mass, especially in the Prayer of the Faithful.

Children grow up and discover that their parents are not almighty after all, and that their love is not perfect. As we mature in the spiritual life we become even more aware of God's power and love. Prayer of petition proclaims that God is our Father and we are his children.

THURSDAY OF THE FIRST WEEK OF LENT (II)

Lent traditionally has been a time dedicated to mortification, almsgiving, and prayer. While all three elements are important, today's liturgical readings emphasize prayer, and specifically prayer of petition.

Queen Esther is proposed as a model for our prayer, even though our circumstances hardly match hers. The background is that Haman, the prime minister of King Xerxes of Persia, contrived a plot to kill in a single day all the Jews living in the Persian Empire. Although she was Jewish, Esther had been chosen queen.

Today's reading contains the prayer which she offered to God before she went in to the king to intercede for her people. She was "taking her life in her hands" because of the law that anyone who approached the king in his inner court without being summoned was subject to death. When the king saw Esther he laid aside the law, listened to her plea, and spared the people.

The lesson is that God is pleased with prayer of petition and is responsive to it. The stakes need not be as high as they were for Esther. The way Jesus speaks in the gospel should make us realize that we are to pray even about ordinary needs and wants.

The essential disposition is to realize that we depend completely on God in every aspect of our lives. The simplicity and directness of Esther's prayer is truly profound: "Lord, help me who am alone and have no help but you."

FRIDAY OF THE FIRST WEEK OF LENT (I)

Sometimes people think that Lent is the time for "less" — less
food and drink, less entertainment, less fun. Another way to
look at Lent is to see it as a time for "more."

If we have been prayerful, then we must become more
prayerful during Lent. If we have been abstemious regarding
food and drink, we must become more abstemious. If we have
been generous in helping others, we must become more
generous.

This simple idea of "more" characterizes the spirit of
Christianity as proclaimed by Jesus in his Sermon on the Mount
(from which today's gospel is taken).

First Jesus tells us that we must be more holy than the
scribes and Pharisees who followed the old law. Murder was
forbidden, but Jesus says that the spirit of "more" overcomes
anger, abusive language, and contempt for another.

Worship expresses our relationship with God as our
Father. Jesus says that the spirit of "more" moves us to be
reconciled with God's children, our brothers and sisters, before
we come to worship.

Sometimes there is less struggle in giving up cigarettes or
liquor or food than there is in being more patient with family
members, more kind to those with whom we work, and more
unselfish in our prayers to God.

The point is that we should never ask "What is the least I
have to do in order to get by?" We should rather ask, "What
more can I do in order to follow the spirit of Christ?"

FRIDAY OF THE FIRST WEEK OF LENT (II)

Ezekiel was called to be a prophet in Babylon where his people were suffering in exile. The people tended to blame their plight on the sins of their fathers and to excuse themselves from any guilt.

Ezekiel condemned this notion of corporate guilt and insisted that each person is responsible for his own sins. He then went a step further. He exposed why the people searched for a reason for their punishment other than their own sins. They were loathe to forgive injuries which others had done them and so, thinking that God was like themselves, they were afraid to admit their guilt. They simply did not believe in the bountiful forgiveness of God.

We should not draw a picture of God which matches our characteristics. We find it very difficult to forgive people who have hurt us deeply. Even when we forgive, we tend not to forget. When something happens to remind us of the old injury, all the feelings of enmity which we thought we had overcome return.

God is not that way. In the sacrament of penance we receive God's absolution. This word, "absolution," is related to the word "absolute," and has the ring of completeness and finality about it.

We need never look for excuses for our sins. We do not have to try to put the blame on other people, on our heredity, or on the environment of modern society. We can be honest and forthright with God because his forgiveness is absolute.

SATURDAY OF THE FIRST WEEK OF LENT (I)

Today's reading from the Book of Deuteronomy invited the people to renew their relationship with the Lord. It should make us realize that in every Mass we are invited to renew our relationship with God.

The old covenant was an agreement with the people that the Lord would be their God and they would "walk in his ways and observe his statutes, commandments, and decrees." That may sound a little legalistic, like a contract, but the relationship between the Lord and his people was actually a covenant. A contract is binding by law, but a covenant is binding by love. The covenant mediated through Moses was based on God's incomprehensible love.

Someone started the idea that the Old Testament was one of fear and the New Testament is one of love. Such an interpretation results from a feeble attempt to grasp the fullness of God's love as manifested to us in Christ; nonetheless, the idea is false. God was, is, and always will remain a God of love.

As we struggle to understand the immensity of God's love, we are not too far from the truth when we see our new covenant in Christ as greater than the old. In Christ we witness an unfolding of God's love. Saints and scholars have not been able to imagine a relationship with God which is drawn from a deeper love than the one which Christ established by his death on the cross. This is the covenant we renew in every Mass.

SATURDAY OF THE FIRST WEEK OF LENT (II)

The Old Testament Book of Deuteronomy was addressed to a generation of Israelites who lived long after the events which it presents. And yet the book is composed in such a way that it brings the listeners into the narrative and makes them part of it.

The people heard the Book of Deuteronomy during their liturgy, just as we do during our liturgy. Their belief was that within the liturgy the Word of God took on a current meaning so that those who heard and responded to the Word were drawn into the eternal action of God.

The Book of Deuteronomy has favorite expressions: *"This day* the Lord, your God, commands you to observe these statutes and decrees. . . . *Today* you are making this agreement with the Lord . . . and *today* the Lord is making this agreement with you."

The expression "this day" or "today" indicates what scholars call the liturgical "now." Liturgy makes things happen. Pope Pius XII taught that the "liturgical year is not a cold and lifeless representation of the past. . . . It is rather Christ himself who is living in his Church . . . and whose mysteries are ever present and active (in the liturgy)" (*Mediator Dei*, 165).

This means that the scriptures in the liturgy are more than an historical record; they are a proclamation addressed to us now, today. When we hear the expression from the gospel "Jesus said to his disciples," we must realize that we are the disciples and Jesus is speaking to us.

MONDAY OF THE SECOND WEEK OF LENT (I)

Today's first reading from the Book of Daniel is unusual in that it is a prayer addressed to God and not a proclamation addressed to us. The community, speaking through Daniel, acknowledged its guilt as a cause of the exile which they were suffering.

This prayer serves as a model for our Lenten spirit of repentance. In accord with this spirit we should resolve to celebrate the sacrament of penance before Easter.

The first step is a frank examination of our lives. Honesty with God is the best policy. There is no possibility of hiding our sins from God as we might from each other, nor is there need to do so. God does not lie in wait to pounce upon us in order to throttle us for our sins; rather he invites us to accept his forgiving embrace.

The second step is to tell God our sincere sorrow and our purpose of amendment. Contrition is best expressed in a firm resolution to accept God's grace to avoid sin in the future. We may fear that we will not succeed perfectly, but we should never stop trying.

The third step is to participate in the sacrament of penance, preferably a "penance service," before the conclusion of Lent. In answer to his prayer Daniel heard consoling words from the angel Gabriel. We hear the forgiving words of Christ spoken by the priest: "May God give you pardon and peace, and I absolve you from your sins."

MONDAY OF THE SECOND WEEK OF LENT (II)

Some people love to hand out advice, but those who do not practice what they preach win neither our confidence nor our respect. A doctor who tells you to quit smoking while a cigarette dangles from his lips is not the kind of physician you trust.

Jesus in today's gospel is rather free with his advice. In fact his words are stronger than advice; they are actually imperatives: "Be compassionate, do not judge, do not condemn, pardon, give."

These are strong words but we accept them because they contain a spirit which Jesus practiced as well as preached. He was compassionate to the sick. He left judgment to his heavenly Father. He refused to condemn the woman who was caught in adultery. He pardoned those who conspired to kill him, and he gave his life on the cross for our salvation as his ultimate gift.

During Lent we are called to repentance, which means to turn away from sin and toward goodness. As we listen to the sacred scriptures which are part of the daily Masses of Lent, we will hear much advice and many exhortations from both the Old and the New Testament readings. In each instance we will find upon reflection that Jesus has fulfilled what we are urged to do. He confirms and illustrates the words of sacred scripture with his actions. He is not only our teacher; he is our supreme model.

TUESDAY OF THE SECOND WEEK OF LENT (I)

Today's gospel seems to be one which we do not follow in practice. Jesus said rather sternly, "Do not call anyone on earth your father." And yet we give this title both to male parents and to priests.

Jesus also said, "Avoid being called teacher or rabbi." These titles, father, teacher, and rabbi, amounted to the same thing. They were honored names bestowed by a tradition among the Jews which valued a knowledge of the Word of God.

What Jesus objected to was a pride on the part of those to whom these titles were granted, as if they represented personal excellence. For example, lawyers in our courts address the judge as "Your honor," not because they want to flatter him and gain his favor, but because lawyers are expected to respect his office and our legal system.

Jesus in fact told the people to obey the scribes and the Pharisees, despite their unworthiness. He recognized that they held the authority of Moses.

In the Christian community we are called to look beyond individuals, not just to a legal system or a human authority, but to the person of Christ. Any teacher who guides students to the truth manifests Christ who is the truth. Any parent or priest who shows forth love and concern manifests Christ who is the image of the Father.

Do we follow today's gospel? Yes, if we acknowledge Christ in the titles of respect which we give to each other.

TUESDAY OF THE SECOND WEEK OF LENT (II)

Isaiah warned his people that rituals of worship are hollow without an expression in virtuous living. Prayer without morality is worthless.

To shock his hearers into attention he addressed them as "princes of Sodom" and "people of Gomorrah." These cities symbolized depravity. It was like calling someone today a willful pervert and a pusher of drugs.

After getting the attention of the people with the bad news of their behavior, Isaiah presented them with the good news of God's mercy. In a colorful image Isaiah proclaimed in the name of the Lord: "Come now, let us set things right. Though your sins be like scarlet, they may become white as snow; though they be crimson red, they may become white as wool."

Despite our dedication to prayer and the Mass, we may find that we are not always the kind of people we should be. Sometimes despite our best intentions, we see ourselves falling back into old habits or the usual sins. Even if our failures are not quite scarlet or crimson, we may be a little black and blue from the struggle. That bad news can be discouraging.

The good news is that God is always merciful. He is eager to set things right. In the sacrament of penance we hear the consoling words, "Through the ministry of the Church may God give you pardon and peace." By means of sacramental absolution scarlet becomes white as snow and crimson red becomes white as wool.

WEDNESDAY OF THE SECOND WEEK OF LENT (I)

We all have our favorite way of doing things. Some people love to settle down with the Sunday newspaper and go through it section by section. The older we become, the more set we become in our ways.

God has his favorite way of doing things. Although we cannot speak of God as becoming older, perhaps there is something about his eternal quality which suggests that he is "set in his ways."

During Lent the Church emphasizes the paschal mystery. It is God's way of doing things. For Jesus this meant that the Father led him through suffering to joy, through humiliation to glory, and through death to life.

Jesus presented the paschal mystery to the disciples when he explained that he would go up to Jerusalem to be crucified, but that on the third day he would be raised up. It was a pattern which God had been following all along.

When the Israelites became slaves in Egypt, God led them forth in the exodus from slavery to freedom. After the Jews had been taken to Babylon in exile, God continued his way of doing things. From the slavery of Babylon he brought them back to Jerusalem and reshaped them in their Jewish identity.

As God dealt with his Son and the people who went before him, so will he deal with us who follow his Son. Christ has died, and so will we; Christ has been raised, and so will we.

WEDNESDAY OF THE SECOND WEEK OF LENT (II)

During Lent the Church emphasizes the paschal mystery. Jesus was thinking of this mystery when he explained to his disciples that he would go up to Jerusalem to suffer and to die, but that on the third day he would be raised up.

For Jesus the paschal mystery was realized when God the Father led him through suffering to joy, through humiliation to glory, and through death to life.

Jesus, though a single person, gathers together into himself all the people of God — he "recapitulates" us in himself. By looking at Christ we can see how the paschal mystery applies to ourselves.

The paschal mystery does not mean, to put it in a common way, that God beats us over the head because it feels so good when he stops. Rather there is a connection of cause and effect. God the Father exalted his Son in the resurrection precisely because he became obedient unto death, even death on a cross.

Zebedee's sons missed the point when, through their mother, they asked to have places of honor in the kingdom. They wanted to partake of the banquet without drinking from the cup of suffering. They wanted the resurrection without the cross.

If they had reflected on the lives of people who had gone before them, such as Jeremiah (first reading), they would have been prepared for Jesus' teaching. We are called to reflect on Jesus himself so that we may share fully in the paschal mystery.

THURSDAY OF THE SECOND WEEK OF LENT (I)

Today's parable condemns a rich man. What was his crime? There is no suggestion in the story that he had acquired his wealth dishonestly or that he had deprived others of their livelihood. He could have asked, "What have I done wrong?" The point is that he did nothing. He completely ignored Lazarus, the poor man who lay at his gate. His sin was not one of commission; it was one of omission.

The sad part of the parable is that the rich man had the means to help Lazarus. He could have assisted him out of the abundance of his wealth which he could not have consumed in a lifetime.

During the penitential rite of the Mass when we use the "I confess," we admit that we have sinned through our own fault in what we have done and in what we have failed to do. We are guilty of sins of commission and sins of omission. Perhaps we need to reflect on our sins of omission.

Our society is filled with indigent people. Every city and town has its homeless and its hungry. In every neighborhood there are shut-ins, the handicapped, and the elderly. If Lazarus is not at our doorstep, he is around the corner or up the block.

We do not have to be wealthy to help those in need. Jesus wants us to give what we have: our attention, our time, and our love.

THURSDAY OF THE SECOND WEEK OF LENT (II)

With profound wisdom the prophet Jeremiah today declares, "More tortuous than all else is the human heart." The word "tortuous" means twisting and turning, but there is a sound to it which suggests torture or pain. When it comes to the human heart, both ideas apply.

This is what tortuous is like. You are climbing a mountain. You have a trail to follow, but it is twisting and turning. At times you feel you are not making progress as you move sideways along the face of the mountain. Then you slip and skin your knees and elbows as you slide down the face of the mountain. You reach out for something to stop your fall. Then you pull yourself together, look to the top, and start your journey again.

More tortuous than all else is the human heart. We are climbing toward God but sometimes we slip back and turn our attention to someone or something other than God. We may love some person selfishly, greedily, possessively. But nothing is worse than loving ourselves, to want our way, our comfort, our convenience, no matter what. Such was the mistake of the rich man in the gospel. He was not mean. He was simply so absorbed in himself that he did not even notice the poor man at his door.

Lent is the time to straighten out our hearts, to look to the top of the mountain, and to keep our eyes fixed on the end of the journey.

FRIDAY OF THE SECOND WEEK OF LENT (I)

I imagine that most of us think of ourselves as non-violent persons. We are shocked by the fictional violence on television and the actual violence in our streets. And even though we recognize that family squabbles are almost inevitable, it is hard to imagine how Joseph's brothers could have been so cruel to him. Their hatred was so fierce that only Reuben's intervention prevented Joseph's murder.

It is even harder to imagine how someone could have pounded nails into the hands and feet of Jesus. How insensitive his executioners must have been to carry out his crucifixion. How hard hearted must have been his enemies who plotted this cruel death.

The idea of physically attacking and harming another person is repulsive, but there is another way of doing damage. When some of us were kids, we used to chant, "Sticks and stones may break my bones, but names will never harm me." Not so. There are things more harmful to others than sticks and stones, such as ruining people's reputations, excluding them from our company, talking about them behind their back, or making fun of them to their face.

That kind of cruelty causes real damage and deep pain to people who are our spiritual brothers and sisters. You can harm people without throwing them into a cistern, and you can crucify them without nailing them to a cross.

FRIDAY OF THE SECOND WEEK OF LENT (II)

In many movies and novels you can pretty well guess what the ending will be. When God is at work, the outcome is very often the opposite of what you expect. There is an irony in God's way of acting.

When Joseph's brothers sold him into slavery, they thought that they were rid of him at last. In no way did they suspect that God would raise Joseph to power in Egypt and that he would become the savior of his brothers during a great famine. Their act of hatred and separation was used by God to bring about love and reunion.

The son in today's gospel parable who was murdered by the tenant farmers represents Jesus. The parable became a reality when Jesus was crucified, but again God was at work. One would have thought that the crucifixion was surely the end of our relationship with God. Just the opposite is true.

The crucifixion, despite appearances, was a death which Jesus freely accepted. He opened his arms on the cross to embrace the entire human race and to win for his Father a new people, a new family.

Although Jesus was rejected, he became the keystone of the structure which is the Church. Within the Church we are brothers and sisters of one another because we have all become sons and daughters of one Father, God himself. Through the death of God's Son we all became God's children.

The divine irony manifests God's mysterious love for us.

SATURDAY OF THE SECOND WEEK OF LENT (I)

Today's gospel is known as the parable of the prodigal son, and yet it has been frequently observed that the story is really about neither of the sons. It is about the father who represents God.

The younger son left home and became prodigal or wasteful of his inheritance. When he returned home in repentance, the father welcomed him and ordered a celebration in joyful thanksgiving.

The older son, when he realized that his father had welcomed his younger brother back home, refused to go in to the celebration. Then the father did an amazing thing: he went out to the son and pleaded with him to join the celebration. The extraordinary character of the father was such that he refused to take sides. He loved both boys simply because they were his sons and he wanted reconciliation between them. That is the way God is.

In order to help bring about reconciliation in the Church today, we must learn to identify with the father. There are some Catholics who resent the changes brought about by Vatican II and who even at times seek illicit forms of the Mass. They are like the older son. Others care little or nothing for tradition and regulations and want to celebrate Mass in overly individualistic ways or abandon the Mass altogether. They are like the younger son.

We must be like the father, never rejecting anyone, but always offering a loving welcome to all our brothers and sisters.

SATURDAY OF THE SECOND WEEK OF LENT (II)

Today's gospel is known as the parable of the prodigal son because Jesus painted a very vivid and realistic picture of that young man. But there are three characters in the story. God is represented by the father. Some of us are represented by the older son and some of us, by the younger son. In many instances there is a bit of both children in all of us.

We need to pay attention to the wishes of the father. When the younger son came back home, the father said, "Let us eat and celebrate because this son of mine was dead and has come back to life."

When the older son rejected the celebration, his father went out and pleaded with him to come in. He explained, "We must celebrate and rejoice."

That is what God says to us: "We must celebrate and rejoice." The Mass is the offering of the victim whose death has reconciled us to God and one another. It is not intended to be a dull ritual. It is not an individualistic act of piety. It is the joyful celebration of our reunion with God and one another.

God the Father has not killed the fatted calf for us. Rather he offers us his own divine Son. That is why we pray: "May all of us who share in the body and blood of Christ be brought together in unity by the Holy Spirit."

The Mass is the family restored. We must celebrate and rejoice!

"It is important to impress on the minds of the faithful not only the social consequences of sin but also that the real essence of the virtue of penance is hatred for sin as an offense against God. The role of the Church in penitential practices is not to be passed over, and the people must be exhorted to pray for sinners" *(Constitution on the Sacred Liturgy, 110).*

OPTIONAL MASS FOR THE THIRD WEEK OF LENT

Both readings of this Mass possess a richness of content, but the Church during Lent is interested primarily in what they suggest about water, which is the sacramental sign of baptism.

In a former era baptism was by immersion. The catechumens were lowered beneath the water as a sign of dying to sin and to a former way of life, and they were lifted up from the water as a sign that they were being raised to a new life in Christ. The action was performed three times to symbolize that through Christ the baptized were entering into the life of the Trinity. Baptism is a transition from death to life in God.

Even without immersion, water is a sign of both death and life. After their escape from Egypt the Israelites complained about a lack of water in the desert, since without water they were bound to die.

After Jesus asked the Samaritan woman for a drink, he said to her, "If only you recognized God's gift, and who it is that is asking you for a drink, you would have asked him instead, and he would have given you living water."

The Church asks Jesus for the living water which saves us from death and gives us the gift of eternal life in baptism. During Lent we all need to grow in our appreciation of this sacrament. Every drop of water we drink should remind us of this gracious gift from God.

MONDAY OF THE THIRD WEEK OF LENT (I)

An abiding, but unfair, story about doctors is that if you call one on the phone at night about an illness, he will tell you to take two aspirins and call him in the morning.

Naaman's illness was leprosy. Being told to wash in the Jordan was like being told to take two aspirins. There was nothing spectacular about washing in the Jordan.

Do we at times look for something spectacular regarding our faith? Some people spend a lot of money in order to travel a long distance at no little inconvenience to a remote location where they judge themselves blessed to kneel near the spot where someone says Our Lady appeared. And yet in any Catholic church can be found the sacrifice of the Mass and the abiding sacramental presence of the Lord of life. We can be certain that Mary is pleased to have us share in the Mass just as she stood at the foot of the cross.

An ordinary weekday Mass gives us the opportunity to participate in something which, even though not spectacular, is the greatest act on this earth. Pope Pius XII wrote in 1947: "All the faithful ought to be aware that to participate in the eucharistic sacrifice is their chief duty and their supreme dignity" (*Mediator Dei*, 80).

When Naaman agreed to do a simple thing, he was cured. When we appreciate even a simple Mass, we are people who are blessed indeed.

MONDAY OF THE THIRD WEEK OF LENT (II)

No matter how extraordinary something may be, once it becomes familiar we tend to take it for granted. People used to marvel at the "miracle" of television and jet travel, but no more. They have become commonplace.

Jesus had this human reaction in mind when he observed that "No prophet gains acceptance in his native place." When he came back to his boyhood home of Nazareth, the people rejected him because he was familiar to them.

It has often been observed that converts make very good Catholics because they appreciate their faith, whereas cradle Catholics tend to take it all for granted. We can take a step toward a deeper appreciation of our faith by imagining what life would be like without it.

Without faith the crucifixion would look like a failure, and all the sayings of Jesus would have no more meaning than the reflections of a forgotten rabbi or an obscure prophet.

Without faith we would have no Church, no eucharist, and no hope for eternal life. We would be but little better than the dumb animals who found nothing of note in the crib of Bethlehem and who wandered off into the night to look for some food and a little warmth against the cold night air.

But through faith, instead of being like the animals, we are like Mary, dedicated to the person of her Son with the conviction that he is our Lord and Savior who gives meaning and purpose to our lives.

TUESDAY OF THE THIRD WEEK OF LENT (I)

Today's parable is not true to life. When the king's servant was unable to pay off his huge debt, he pleaded for more time. The king granted even more than he asked and wrote off the debt.

Creditors do not act that way. The bank is not going to write off your debt no matter how hard you plead. The king is like no one we know—except God.

And that is the point. God is different from us. Where we are petty, God is big. Where we are greedy, God is generous. Where we are unforgiving, God absolves us from our sins.

Jesus presents God's forgiveness as a motive for us to forgive each other. When he says that we are to forgive seventy times seven times, he does not mean that after four hundred and ninety acts of forgiveness we may become hardened. There should be no limit as to how often we forgive, nor is there to be a limit as to how completely we forgive. That is the meaning of "writing off the debt."

Jesus exemplified this kind of forgiveness. We should not be surprised if we find it difficult to imitate him. After all, we are trying to rise above our human limitations and to be like Jesus himself. The only means is to open ourselves to the power of the holy eucharist. Through receiving the body and blood of the Lord we can become more like him and grow in his spirit of forgiveness.

TUESDAY OF THE THIRD WEEK OF LENT (II)

After placing the bread and the wine on the altar during the preparation of the gifts, the priest bows and says inaudibly: "Lord, God, we ask you to receive us and be pleased with the sacrifice we offer you with humble and contrite hearts."

Today's first reading is the source of this prayer. It is a plea for mercy from God within the context of an honest admission by the community that their sufferings have been brought on by their sins.

Since the people were deprived of the temple and the opportunity to offer liturgical sacrifices, they asked God to accept their sufferings in place of the sacrifices of the temple.

Within the Mass our sentiment is somewhat different. Our sacrifice is the body of Christ given up for us and his blood poured out for us. We do not ask God to accept our sufferings in place of a liturgical sacrifice; rather, we join our sufferings with those of Christ as he makes present on the altar the offering of himself in sacrifice to the Father.

But there is more. We should remember to offer our joys as well as our sorrows. In fact, we are invited to offer our entire beings.

Our sentiment during the eucharistic prayer should be this: "Father, we ask you to receive us in union with your Son, for then we know that you will be pleased with the sacrifice we offer you with humble and contrite hearts."

WEDNESDAY OF THE THIRD WEEK OF LENT (I)

Good parents try to determine what is best for their sons and daughters and set up rules in accord with that judgment. They forbid some actions because they are harmful and command others because they are beneficial.

Children often look upon the rules of their parents as limitations of their freedom. They want to be able to do what they want, to skip homework and to stay up late watching television, to go out with kids of their choice, whether their parents think they are a good influence or not, and to give in to the peer pressure which urges them to experiment with drugs.

It is difficult for children to see that their parents make rules only because they love them and want the best for them. That is understandable for children. Sometimes, however, adults react childishly toward God and his commandments. A mature person ought to see in God's commandments a clear sign of his wisdom and his love.

Parents can make mistakes in regard to their children. God cannot. That is why Moses said regarding God's commandments, "Observe them carefully, for thus you will give evidence of your wisdom and intelligence."

One reason we come to Mass is to receive the strength we need to embrace God's will in our lives. We find that strength in holy communion. We receive the body and blood of Christ who prayed to his Father as a dutiful son, "Not my will, but yours be done."

WEDNESDAY OF THE THIRD WEEK OF LENT (II)

In the military a number of regulations are made only in order to develop discipline. Actions are wrong simply because they are forbidden. Parents, on the other hand, forbid some actions because they are wrong or harmful.

God does not work either way. God does not dream up rules in order to make us people of character, or forbid something as a test. Nor does he search for what is good as parents do. Rather he makes the good to be good. God does not command something because it is right. Rather his will is what makes something to be right. Anything not in accord with his will is evil by its nature and forbidden in itself. That is why Jesus tells us that God's law will never pass away since God himself cannot pass away.

We are right in judging that the precepts of the Church possess a value because they express in human terms God's divine will. In some situations God's will is clear to us. In others it is not. No matter how many commandments and precepts we have, they do not always cover every human situation nor is it always easy to apply these regulations correctly.

Finding and following God's will in every instance is a lifelong process, but nothing less will bring us happiness. That is why we pray every day at Mass in the Lord's prayer, "Thy will be done on earth as it is in heaven."

THURSDAY OF THE THIRD WEEK OF LENT (I)

When Jesus was accused of casting out devils by the power of the prince of devils, he pointed out the absurdity of this attack upon him. He was doing good things, but Satan does not cooperate with good. For him to do so would be to foster a civil war within his own domain.

That is what Jesus had in mind when he observed that a kingdom divided against itself is weakened from within and is easily laid waste by its enemies. Satan was too smart to be self-destructive by being in league with Jesus.

All our hope is in Jesus. For us not to choose him is to be self-destructive. Jesus insisted that the choice must be definite: we cannot be partly for Jesus and partly against him. Nor is indifference acceptable: the person who is not with Jesus is against him.

And yet we must be honest and admit that at times we waver. We are not always and everywhere perfectly in accord with the teachings of Jesus. We are weak and we make mistakes. We have the best intentions but we cannot easily overcome bad habits. When we go to confession, we possibly find that we confess the same sins over and over. Our soul is like a house divided.

Jesus is stronger than our weaknesses. To him we come in holy communion and pray: Lord, take possession of our house. Dwell therein and cast out all evil from our heart and soul.

THURSDAY OF THE THIRD WEEK OF LENT (II)

When children play games, everyone hopes to be chosen for the right team. What is really bad is to be ignored and not chosen at all. But being chosen for the right team is not enough. The players have to act together and follow the captain.

Some of the Israelites, though chosen by God, failed to follow him, their captain. God complained about them: "They turned their backs, not their faces to me. This is the nation which does not listen to the voice of the Lord, its God, or take correction." Their pride and selfishness got in the way of their teamwork.

Through the sacrament of baptism God placed his hand on our shoulder and said, "I choose you." He selected us to be on his side. He said to us, "I am your God. You are my people." We said, "We renounce Satan," the captain of the other team.

Life is not a game we play. And yet there are aspects of life which are not unlike the games we played as children.

We must work together now: no pride, no selfishness. The only star on our team is the captain, who is Jesus. A captain has to take the lead and is usually the best player. We have that confidence in Jesus.

Above all we must remember that we have been chosen for the winning team. We must not frustrate that choice by God.

FRIDAY OF THE THIRD WEEK OF LENT (I)

Jesus would not have done well in academic examinations. He almost never answered a question directly or in accord with what was asked.

In today's gospel he was asked, "What is the first of all the commandments?" To that question there should be only one answer, but Jesus gave two. In fact he quoted two distinct books of the Old Testament. His first answer is from the Book of Deuteronomy (6:44); his second is from the Book of Leviticus (19:18).

Jesus refused to give one answer because true love for God cannot be separated from love for people. "Whoever loves God must also love his brothers and sisters" (1 John 4:21).

The sign of peace at Mass reminds us that we cannot separate love for God from love for his people. Before we receive Christ in communion we are asked to manifest love for each other. We cannot really embrace Christ in the eucharist if we reject him in people. Those who do not love their brothers and sisters whom they see cannot love the God whom they do not see (cf. 1 John 4:20).

When we come before the Lord in judgment, he will ask, "Have you kept the great commandment?" We will say, "Yes, Lord, we have loved you with all our heart, all our soul, and all our mind, and all our strength." And the Lord will say, "I am sorry but I cannot accept only one answer to my question."

FRIDAY OF THE THIRD WEEK OF LENT (II)

Lent is a time for conversion, for turning to God in love. We hear the words of Hosea, "Return, O Israel, to the Lord your God," and we apply them to ourselves because conversion is an ongoing experience.

To love God with our whole being is a perfection which is not achieved in an instant. Each day we must try to deepen our love for God.

The prophet Hosea suggests that one of the most beautiful expressions of love is trust. When a person we love asks us to do a favor, we do not say, "Wait a minute. What do you expect in return?" We trust someone we love, and so we should trust God when he asks us to do his will.

When we do not hear from a loved one for weeks on end, we do not think that this person no longer cares about us. We trust that there is a good reason for a lack of communication, and we are confident that our relationship has not faded. Love calls us to trust God even when he seems far away and uncommunicative.

A friend may say, "I have to tell you about something which you really should not be doing." We do not think that he is mean to us or wants to hurt us. We trust him, just as we must trust God when he seems to admonish us.

Love overcomes doubts. Love thinks the best. Love is confident. A beautiful expression of love is trust.

SATURDAY OF THE THIRD WEEK OF LENT (I)

The Pharisee described in today's parable was a professional man of religion. He boasted about his religious observances of fasting and tithing. He protested that he was not grasping, crooked, or adulterous. But he did not receive approval from Jesus. What did he do wrong?

He was an idolater who worshipped himself. He believed in his own self-righteousness. He actually thought that he had accomplished everything by himself. He was, in his own view, a self-made man and he was proud of his creation.

Notice that the Pharisee asked nothing from God, not even mercy, because he was convinced that he needed nothing. He was complete unto himself. He refused to let God be God.

On the other hand, the tax collector claimed nothing as his own except his sins. That is why he turned to the Lord and pleaded, "O God, be merciful to me a sinner." He was not pleased with himself, but he had faith that God would not reject him. He knew that a contrite spirit is a sacrifice pleasing to God.

Each day as we prepare to celebrate the sacrifice of the Mass, we ask God for mercy. With the tax collector we strike our breast and say, "O God, be merciful to me, a sinner." It is perhaps the most honest moment of the day. It is a confession of our weakness and our need for the Lord. It is our way of letting God be God.

SATURDAY OF THE THIRD WEEK OF LENT (II)

At times in history people have seen the Lord as a God of inexorable wrath; at other times they have seen him as a God of indulgent permissiveness.

The prophet Hosea was concerned about the people of his day. Their attitude was, "Don't bother about God. He is punishing us now, but he will come around in a day or two and we won't have a thing to worry about." They thought it was enough to mouth a few pious prayers of repentance, nothing too serious, and let it go at that. They saw God as a permissive parent who might threaten his children but who ends up spoiling them.

God was not pleased. Through Hosea he complained that the piety of the people was like the dew on the ground which quickly evaporates. Because of his love he wanted to forgive his people, but he required sincerity.

We need a balanced attitude toward God. We should not fear to approach God to ask forgiveness as if he were a tyrannical ogre, nor should we simply ignore his commandments as if he were a tolerant weakling who would never dream of punishing us.

Jesus in the parable today gives us a model. The tax collector was sincere when he said, "O God be merciful to me, a sinner." He made no excuses. He was honest before the Lord. Jesus assures us that our sincere, honest efforts toward repentance will be favored by our loving God.

"During Lent penance should not be only internal and individual but also external and social. The practice of penance should be fostered according to the possibilities of the present day and of a given area, as well as of specific circumstances."

(*Constitution on the Sacred Liturgy*, 110)

OPTIONAL MASS FOR THE FOURTH WEEK OF LENT

The episode about the man who was born blind is both striking and unique. According to the gospel story, the blind man did not cry out to Jesus and ask for a cure as did so many others who were crippled or leprous. Since he was born blind, he really had no way of grasping his deprivation. Jesus took the initiative.

What a startling, exciting experience it must have been for this man to have seen for the first time as an adult. We can be quite sure he never forgot Jesus or what he did for him on this day.

The Church traditionally reads this gospel in connection with the sacrament of baptism. Jesus, seeing us blinded by sin, has taken the initiative. Through baptism he has given us a new vision through faith whereby he has become the light of our life. Infants who are baptized have no understanding of what is lacking to them without this sacrament, and so they have no appreciation of its meaning. But even after we grow up, we cannot comprehend either the darkness of life without Christ or the immensity of the gift of baptism.

The season of Lent concentrates on baptism and culminates with either its celebration for catechumens or its renewal for the faithful. The hope is that we will deepen our appreciation of baptism and come to a greater sense of its value. The Lord is truly our light and our salvation.

MONDAY OF THE FOURTH WEEK OF LENT (I)

The Galileans looked upon Jesus as a hometown boy who was gaining a reputation because of the cures he had accomplished. They were somewhat like a young man who is attracted to a young woman only because of her beauty. The woman hopes that the man will come to know her as a person and to realize that, as we say, her beauty is more than skin deep.

Jesus worked a life-giving miracle for the royal official whose son was ill. He saw in the official a man who had a limited faith but who was open to God's grace. His judgment was not misplaced. Once the official returned home to find that his son was going to live, he and his whole household became believers.

We should see in the official a model of true faith which leads to commitment. That kind of faith goes beyond the surface, as true love sees beyond external beauty to the person.

In baptism Jesus gave us the seed of everlasting life, and he nourishes this seed through the holy eucharist. These sacraments of life are wonderful gifts, greater than the miracle granted to the royal official, but they are incomplete if we do not allow them to move us to a firm commitment to the person of Jesus Christ. During Lent Jesus invites us to deepen our faith by going beyond the superficial in our relationship with him.

MONDAY OF THE FOURTH WEEK OF LENT (II)

Much of life is taken up with thoughts about the future. Little children in school yearn for holidays, older students plan for graduation, young spouses look forward to the birth of their child, and older couples await the time of retirement.

Although the future may at times hold something unpleasant or even tragic, the human spirit is usually undaunted in hoping for the best.

The first reading today was proclaimed to the people who were the first to return from captivity in Babylon. It was a message which promised a bright future, and yet after the exile they endured much frustration, pain, and sorrow. What they did not clearly understand was that their freedom from slavery was the prelude of something even greater to come in Christ.

That something is freedom from slavery to sin and slavery to eternal death, a freedom won by the paschal sacrifice of Christ.

Easter Sunday will be for us a fulfillment and a promise. We will experience the grace of renewed life in Christ, but it will be only a prelude to the fullness of life that will be ours on the day of resurrection. Even after Easter Sunday we will still face frustration, pain and sorrow, but we must never be daunted in our hope. We look forward in faith to a bright future of everlasting life. That is why as one of our eucharistic acclamations we cry out, "Lord, by your cross and resurrection you have set us free; you are the Savior of the world."

TUESDAY OF THE FOURTH WEEK OF LENT (I)

Everyone knows that water is necessary for life, but people who live in a desert are likely to appreciate it more than others.

The priest and prophet, Ezekiel, wrote for a people whose homeland was a desert. When he looked for an image to visualize the abundance of God's love, he was understandably inspired to think of an abundance of water. It was an impressive image for his people.

But water, even in abundance, is not sufficient by itself. It must be the right kind of water. In Coleridge's poem, the Ancient Mariner complained, "Water, water, everywhere, / And all the boards did shrink; / Water, water, everywhere, / Nor any drop to drink." If he had drunk the salt water which surrounded him, it would only have intensified his thirst. He needed "sweet" water.

We have what may be called "sweet water" in the sacrament of baptism. Because the ceremony is simple, and for most of us took place when we were infants, we may be inclined to take its meaning for granted. Even if we were tiny and only a trickle of water flowed over our forehead, a big thing happened to us. The water was a sign of our dying to sin and rising to new life in Christ. The abundance of God's love was poured out upon us.

During Lent the liturgy calls us to appreciate the great gift of our baptism so that we may never take it for granted.

TUESDAY OF THE FOURTH WEEK OF LENT (II)

Jesus in an instant cured a man who had been sick for thirty-eight years. The man's joy must have been electric, and one would think that those who witnessed the cure would have been happy for him. But there was a problem. The day was a sabbath when no work was permitted, and the authorities judged that the cure violated the law of absolute rest.

I suspect that we have a hard time not only understanding why the interpretation of the law was so strict but also why anyone for whatever reason would object to a miracle of compassion which Jesus had performed. In fact it is abhorrent to us that anyone should oppose Jesus for any reason. And yet it was because Jesus did such things on the sabbath that the authorities began to persecute him. What a flimsy reason!

Perhaps we need to reflect on some possible failures of our own. Are we inclined to judge harshly the motives of those who do good for others, to resent the attention they receive, or to complain that they do not do things our way? Do we come to the liturgy with a critical spirit which is like that with which the authorities viewed Jesus? Do we manufacture flimsy reasons for a lack of generosity?

If we are not cautious we may end up being rather like those authorities who opposed Jesus. Such a possibility, even in small matters, should be completely abhorrent to us.

WEDNESDAY OF THE FOURTH WEEK OF LENT (I)

Irony can be a dangerous device since the meaning intended is the opposite of the usual sense of the words or actions. And yet God the Father has chosen to employ a divine irony regarding his Son.

The leaders of the people became determined to kill Jesus because he spoke of God as his own Father. The irony is that it was precisely through his death that the identity of Jesus was revealed. God the Father embraced his Son in death and exalted him in his resurrection. As he gave his Son life in the timelessness of eternity, so he restored life to him in the moment of the resurrection.

By giving life to Jesus God manifests that he is his Father. The paschal mystery of the death and resurrection manifests that Jesus is God's Son.

This irony was lost on the Jewish authorities. We must grasp its meaning since it applies to us.

During Lent we are called to repentance and self-denial. Repentance is a way of turning ourselves around so that we face God directly. This repentance leads to self-denial which is a form of death. These are not negative actions, even though they appear as such to people without faith. The irony is that by turning away from ourselves to face God, we discover our true identity as his children. By denying ourselves we come to the fulfillment of our being.

In the divine plan suffering leads to glory and death leads to everlasting life.

WEDNESDAY OF THE FOURTH WEEK OF LENT (II)

A mother's love for her infant is a powerful, natural instinct which is strengthened by a human appreciation for the link between her child and herself. That is why, when the people in captivity felt abandoned by God, he asked them, "Can a mother forget her infant or be without tenderness for the child of her womb?"

This comparison is one of the most touching expressions of God's love in the entire Bible. And yet we know from the sad experience of abortion that a mother can forget her infant. We recognize from the facts of child abuse that a mother can be without tenderness for the child of her womb.

These distressing facts make us realize that no human comparison is adequate to express divine love. But our only way of knowing God, apart from direct infusion of knowledge, is by comparing him with what we know from our experience.

The result is that we have inadequate views of God. When we offend him, we are afraid that he may turn his back on us the way some friends react when we disturb or hurt them. We may remember, for example, how our boss blew up when we asked for a raise.

St. Paul said that "we see now indistinctly as in a mirror" (1 Cor 13:12). To know God as he is, we must wait for heaven, for that beatific vision when we will see him face to face.

THURSDAY OF THE FOURTH WEEK OF LENT (I)

When we listen to the recorded words of Jesus, especially as they are found in today's gospel, we are led to recognize that he spoke as no man speaks because he is not like any man. His pre-eminence flows from his uniqueness.

Jesus was not a philosopher whose wisdom could be learned. Jesus himself is that wisdom. He was not a prophet whose message could be absorbed. He himself is the message.

Our religion is not a system of ideas, even though we have rightly developed our doctrine over the centuries. It is not a moral code of conduct, even though we have rightly codified our norms for human behavior. Our faith is not an "ism," such as theism, deism, capitalism, or communism. Christianity is a person. No one and no idea can substitute for the person of Christ.

Jesus wrote nothing while he was here on this earth. He left that work to his disciples. He bequeathed to us no documents, no declaration of independence, no constitution or bill of rights. He gave us himself ever living and active in his Church.

We must not see Christ as merely some distant figure of history. By his divine power he is among us, hidden perhaps, but truly present under the appearances of bread and wine, in the simplicity of biblical words, and in the humility of the human countenance.

Christianity is the Person of Jesus Christ.

THURSDAY OF THE FOURTH WEEK OF LENT (II)

In today's first reading we observe an extraordinary scene. Perhaps it is shocking to see Moses' boldness before God, but it is disconcerting to think that his boldness was necessary to intercept the wrath of a vengeful God.

Even though the Israelites were the recipients of God's revelation, they had to struggle to grasp what God was telling them. At times they resorted to anthropomorphisms, an attempt to express divine qualities by a parallel with human characteristics. Such attempts have limited application. As with the parables of Jesus, today's first reading, despite its graphic picture, proposes only one point: God is pleased by intercessory prayer.

By the gracious design of God we have been given two gifts. The first is that of faith whereby we become open to receive and accept God's revelation of himself. The second is that of our place in salvation history whereby we live in that era which has been illuminated by the light of the incarnation. For us anthropomorphisms should yield to the witness given by the humanity of Jesus Christ.

We must be dedicated to the prayerful study of the life and words of Jesus in the gospels. He is God's personal revelation in the flesh, the image of the Father. In him and through his words and actions we come to know God. Our knowledge is now imperfect, but it will lead us to that happy vision of God when we behold him face to face.

FRIDAY OF THE FOURTH WEEK OF LENT (I)

Some people have a hard time making up their minds. They find decisions difficult because while they want to keep their options open they allow themselves to be swayed first by one opinion, then by another.

The people who encountered Jesus had a profound decision to make about him. Jesus had caused such a stir that the word was out that he could possibly be the Messiah. That opinion influenced many of the people, but they could not make up their minds about him.

Someone raised an imaginary objection that when the Messiah came, no one would know his origins. It was a case of a self-proclaimed expert, and we get an image of a man whispering behind his hand to his neighbors. He let the group in on his little pocket of information and observed that Jesus could not be the Messiah since he was from Nazareth and was a carpenter turned prophet. This objection spread among the crowd.

The whisperer was wrong: prophecies indicated that the Messiah would come from David's city of Bethlehem, and that is where Jesus was born, even though he grew up in Nazareth.

We have made our decision about Jesus. We accept him as Messiah and Lord. The question is: do we listen to his voice when the Church teaches or do we follow self-proclaimed experts regarding the ethics of sexuality, abortion, social justice, and economics? Is Jesus our Lord and Master, not in theory, but in practice?

FRIDAY OF THE FOURTH WEEK OF LENT (II)

We see in the gospels how the enmity against Jesus developed into a plot to condemn him to a shameful death.

The leaders in effect said, "Let us beset the just one, because he is obnoxious to us; he sets himself against our doings" (first reading). The amazing thing is that Jesus was not a despised foreigner, like the Romans of occupation, or a hated enemy, like the Samaritans. Jesus was a brother, as Abel was brother to Cain.

After Cain had murdered his brother Abel, God demanded of him, "Where is your brother?" He answered, "I do not know. Am I my brother's keeper?" Then God said, "What have you done? Your brother's blood cries out to me from the soil" (Genesis 4:9f).

After Jesus had been crucified, his blood cried out to God, but not for vengeance. It was a plea for mercy to which the Father responded out of love for his Son. That is why there is no reason to blame anyone for the death of Jesus. His crucifixion was God's mysterious way of overcoming sin and of bringing life from death. St. Paul explains, "None of the rulers knew the mystery; if they had known it, they would never have crucified the Lord of glory" (1 Cor 2:8).

To us the mystery has been revealed. Jesus is more than our keeper. He is our Savior and our Lord. By dying he destroyed our death, and by rising he restored our life.

SATURDAY OF THE FOURTH WEEK OF LENT (I)

A name which has gained no popularity whatsoever is "Nicodemus." I have never met nor even heard of a person named Nicodemus. Perhaps there is something unappealing in the sound, but Nicodemus can serve an excellent model for any disciple of Jesus.

We first meet Nicodemus in the gospel of John when he came to Jesus at night. On that occasion he listened to Jesus and received an instruction on baptism. That event changed his life.

In today's gospel we hear Nicodemus speak. He does so boldly in defense of Jesus and on his behalf. He insists that the Pharisees not condemn Jesus without hearing him and knowing the facts. He is convinced that anyone with an open mind will respond to Jesus as he had.

On Good Friday we will see Nicodemus again. It will be the high point of his life. He will act. He will help Joseph of Aramathea take Jesus from the cross. With love he will embrace the body of Jesus given up in sacrifice for us and for our salvation.

Nicodemus shows us the three steps of discipleship. They are to listen to Jesus, to speak on his behalf, and to act by embracing him in love. The high point for us comes when we grasp the meaning of the death of Jesus, daily celebrated in the eucharist, and receive him in communion as our Savior.

SATURDAY OF THE FOURTH WEEK OF LENT (II)

Jeremiah was a man of profound dedication to the Lord and to the mission he had received as an Old Testament prophet. It was not an easy calling. Jeremiah suffered from misunderstandings about his message, resentment against his warnings, and mistrust of his way of life.

By the grace of God Jeremiah remained faithful, even though at times he did not hesitate to complain to the Lord about his heavy burden. What is remarkable about Jeremiah is that he lacked the strong incentive which has been given to us. Because of the era in which he lived, he did not benefit from the teaching and example of Jesus. We can be sure that Jeremiah would have been greatly cheered as well as strengthened if he had known Jesus Christ.

By the grace of God we know Jesus Christ. We have heard his teaching that we must take up our cross daily and follow him. We have seen his example whereby he not only took up his cross but died upon it.

At times like Jeremiah we may complain about the burdens of life. That is understandable. But we must remember that, unlike Jeremiah, we can recognize that we are actually bearing the cross of Christ.

We believe a further truth which was unknown to Jeremiah: for us, as for Jesus in the paschal mystery, sorrow will be turned into joy and death will lead to resurrection and everlasting life.

"The season of Lent is a preparation for the celebration of Easter. The liturgy prepares the catechumens for the celebration of the paschal mystery by the several stages of Christian initiation. It also prepares the faithful, who recall their baptism and do penance in preparation for Easter"
(*Norms for the Liturgical Year Calendar*, 27)

OPTIONAL MASS FOR THE FIFTH WEEK OF LENT

One day we must all leave this life and pass through the awesome dark doors of death. Because the prospect is frightening, the two stories of this Mass are of profound significance. Both manifest power over death, but in distinctive ways.

When the prophet Elisha found that a young boy had died, he first prayed to the Lord. Then he went through a somewhat elaborate ritual after which the boy opened his eyes.

Jesus stood before the tomb of Lazarus, his friend. In contrast to the actions of Elisha, Jesus performed no ritual. He simply cried out, "Lazarus, come out!" Lazarus who had been dead came out alive.

The word of Jesus was powerful in itself. St. John in composing the story hoped that we would remember how he began his gospel: "In the beginning was the Word."

The word of Jesus was strong enough to overcome death, because he is the Word of God. His verbal utterance manifested his divine identity. Jesus is more than a prophet. He is the Word, the Son of God.

We recall the word of Jesus, "The bread I will give is my flesh for the life of the world," and we realize that Jesus who nourishes us is "the resurrection and the life."

These eucharistic words are not idle ones. They are the power of God which will lead us through those dark doors of death to the joys of everlasting life.

MONDAY OF THE FIFTH WEEK OF LENT (A & B Cycles)

In an earlier era of the liturgy the Pope celebrated Mass during Lent at a different church in Rome each day. The church assigned for this day's liturgy was that of Saint Susanna, a virgin who was martyred in an ancient persecution.

The reading from the Old Testament today concerns another Susanna, a chaste wife who was accused unjustly. The gospel today is about a woman who was caught in the act of adultery.

The liturgy brings together three women who were removed in time from each other and who were involved in distinct circumstances. What they have in common is that in each instance God acted on their behalf. It did not matter that the unnamed woman who was caught in adultery was guilty, or that Susanna who was a dedicated wife was innocent, or that Susanna who was a virgin became the victim of a persecution. God does not abandon any of his people who need him.

Susanna the wife needed someone to defend her; she found him in Daniel. The adulterous woman needed someone to forgive her; she found him in Jesus. The martyr needed someone to receive her spirit with loving arms; she found the warm embrace of the Lord in heaven.

Each of us is precious in God's eyes, and he understands our distinctive circumstances. He responds to each of us according to our needs.

MONDAY OF THE FIFTH WEEK OF LENT (C Cycle)

The book of Daniel, from which today's first reading is taken, was composed during a time of bitter persecution a little more than a century and a half before the birth of Christ. It was presented to the Jewish people to strengthen and comfort them in their ordeal. The story of Susanna shows that justice will triumph in the end. She was unjustly accused, but Daniel, like an ancient Perry Mason, came to her rescue at the last moment.

The author of the Book of Daniel, even though inspired by the Holy Spirit, had no idea of how Jesus would fulfill his principle that justice triumphs.

Susanna was spared death, but not Jesus. Susanna did not undergo the penalty for her alleged crime, but Jesus took upon himself the guilt of the world. Susanna's innocence was demonstrated by Daniel's clever tactic; Jesus' divine identity as Son of God was proclaimed in his resurrection from the dead.

The death of Jesus was his vindication. What appeared to be a tragedy was his glorification.

We do not look to someone like Daniel to be our savior. We embrace Jesus. He promises us that no follower of his "shall ever walk in darkness; he shall possess the light of life." That light comes to us from the dawn of Easter Sunday. The resurrection illumines our lives and shows us, no matter what our suffering or frustration may be, that God will raise us to the glory of eternal life.

TUESDAY OF THE FIFTH WEEK OF LENT (I)

The Israelites became embittered during their journey to the promised land, and they complained about what they called "wretched food."

When God sent poisonous snakes among the people, some repented and asked Moses for help. The Lord told Moses to make a bronze serpent and to mount it on a pole. Whoever looked upon it was saved.

St. John in his gospel (3:14ff) explained the meaning of this episode for us. He wrote: "Just as Moses lifted up the serpent in the desert, so must the Son of Man be lifted up, that all who believe may have eternal life in him."

The Book of Numbers says that Moses "mounted" a bronze serpent on a pole. John changed the verb "mounted" to "lifted up." His verb implies glorification. Jesus, lifted up on the cross, was exalted to glory by his Father.

In union with Jesus we too are exalted. By means of this sacrifice Jesus brought healing from sin and victory over death, and granted us the gift of everlasting life.

As we journey through this earthly desert, the Lord feeds us, not with wretched food, but with his own precious body and blood.

The eucharist is his body given up for us and his blood poured out for us. In the Mass we keep our eyes fixed on the Lord and we proclaim the mystery of our faith: "Dying you destroyed our death; rising you restored our life; Lord Jesus, come in glory."

TUESDAY OF THE FIFTH WEEK OF LENT (II)

As Jesus was beginning his public ministry, John the Baptist sent his disciples to ask Jesus, "Are you he who is to come, or do we look for another?"

As Jesus progressed toward the climax of his public ministry, the Pharisees raised much the same question. They demanded of Jesus, "Who are you?"

The question of the identity of Jesus is not an idle one. Who he is makes all the difference. Someone might sign a peace treaty with a warring nation, but the question would have to be posed, "Who is this person who has signed his name? Is he the appropriate authority to represent his country?"

Jesus insisted that his identity would be revealed in his death and resurrection. That is the meaning of his enigmatic statement, "When you lift up the Son of Man, you will realize that I AM." To be lifted up referred both to being lifted up to the cross by his executioners and to being lifted up in glory by God, his Father. In his death and resurrection Jesus is revealed as the Son of God, one with God who is the "Great I AM."

That identity makes all the difference. Through his sacrifice Jesus has reconciled us with the Father. The peace treaty has been signed in his own blood. He is the appropriate person, the true representative of the Father, because he is one with the Father. We look for no other. Jesus is our reconciliation and our peace.

WEDNESDAY OF THE FIFTH WEEK OF LENT (I)

Slavery in the United States came to an end after the Civil War. President Lincoln's Emancipation Proclamation became effective on January 1, 1863, but much blood was shed before the war was ended and a new era of freedom began to unfold.

Jesus had his own emancipation proclamation. He declared: "The truth will set you free." He wanted us to be free from the slavery of sin. His blood was shed to give power and validity to his proclamation, but even his death was only the beginning of a new era of freedom.

To be truly free we must live according to the teaching of Jesus as his disciples. Then we will know the truth which will set us free.

This truth is that we are children of God. Before the Civil War black people in the slave states were born into servitude. Now we have been born into freedom because God is our Father. Our birth through baptism freed us from sin and death and brought us into God's family. No child of God is a slave to sin unless he wants to be.

The price of our freedom was the death of Jesus. It is also our source of strength so that we may be faithful disciples. When we are nourished by the body and the blood of the Lord in communion, we receive a power which can overcome any obstacle to our freedom from sin. As children of God, we can be truly free.

WEDNESDAY OF THE FIFTH WEEK OF LENT (II)

During the second century before Christ the conquering monarch, Antiochus IV, ordered the Jews in Palestine to take part in pagan worship. Death was the penalty for not doing so.

The story of the three young men who refused to worship the golden statue was told to help the people to trust that God would protect those who remain faithful to him.

In the face of our difficulties, we do well to listen to this story from the Book of Daniel, but for us there is more. We can recognize that God's intervention to save the three young men was part of a long history of God's loving actions which reached a culmination in the person of Jesus.

During these last days of Lent we will see in the gospels the unraveling of the circumstances which led to his suffering and death. As we witness these extraordinary events of the passion of the Son of God, we must ask ourselves, "What more could God do to show his loving care for us, his people?"

This sacrifice of Jesus is so important to us that God does more than tell us the story. In the Mass we celebrate the paschal mystery of our salvation. The eucharist is the living memorial of the death and resurrection of Jesus.

A persecuted people were told the story of the three young men. We hear of and actually live the marvelous event of our salvation in Christ.

THURSDAY OF THE FIFTH WEEK OF LENT (I)

St. John the evangelist has been compared to an eagle which
soars to great heights. This image is appropriate, as we see in
today's presentation of Jesus' discourse with his adversaries. If
we envision the scene, we can wonder how his opponents
could have been expected to understand Jesus'
words.

They objected to Jesus: "You are not yet fifty years old.
How can you have seen Abraham?" It was a reasonable
objection since Abraham lived and died many centuries before
the birth of Jesus. Jesus replied, "Before Abraham came to be, I
AM." It was an enigmatic response since it implied that Jesus
had existed before Abraham.

The objectors reacted by picking up stones to throw at
Jesus. They thought he was guilty of blasphemy by making
himself equal to God. The words of Jesus, born on eagle's
wings, had soared over the heads of his listeners up to the
heights of heaven.

Only by the grace of God and through the light of fuller
revelation do we acknowledge that Jesus is the eternal Son of
God. In his divine person as Son of God he does indeed exist,
not only before Abraham, but before all of creation.

As we listen to the gospel we should express our gratitude
that we have been given the grace to embrace Jesus in his full
identity. We do not hurl rocks at him. We offer him homage
and praise, for he is the Lord of our lives.

THURSDAY OF THE FIFTH WEEK OF LENT (II)

Our name is important to us. It becomes identified with our person. Most people would not want someone to tamper with their name, but God went ahead and changed the name of Abram for his own purpose.

The name "Abram" means "the father is exalted." The longer form given by God means "the father of many." Through Abraham God began working out his plan of salvation for the human race.

With Abraham God entered into a covenant, a solemn promise which would not be broken. In fulfillment of that covenant Abraham became the father of the Twelve Tribes of Israel, but there is more. We believe that Abraham is our father in faith. That is how we refer to him in the First Eucharistic Prayer. The reason for that is that Jesus came as the Messiah in fulfillment of the covenant made with Abraham.

When Jesus opened his arms on the cross, he embraced the people of every time and place. In the Second Eucharistic Prayer we proclaim that "in this he fulfilled God's will and won for him a holy people."

We are those people, the spiritual descendants of Abraham. But we do not bear Abraham's name. Rather we bear the name of the Messiah, the Christ. We are called "Christians."

Jesus said that Abraham rejoiced to see his day. So do we since in Jesus the promises made to Abraham were fulfilled. We are the beneficiaries of that fulfillment.

FRIDAY OF THE FIFTH WEEK OF LENT (I)

Modern psychiatry has given us a word which has become part of almost everyone's vocabulary. The word is "paranoid." It refers to a persecution-complex, a feeling that everyone is out to get you.

Someone listening to Jeremiah's complaints might be tempted to say to him, "Don't be paranoid." But paranoia is a delusion, a mentality which is not in accord with reality. No one is really out to get a paranoid person. Such was not the case with Jeremiah. He had very real and very powerful persecutors.

The same was true of Jesus. Amazing though it may seem to us, the leaders of the people were determined not merely to harm Jesus in order to silence him but to kill him in order to be rid of him.

Evil is vehemently and obsessively opposed to good. There is no paranoia in thinking that we face forceful obstacles in our efforts to be holy people. We have enemies as surely as did Jeremiah and Jesus himself. We can identify some of these enemies as certain traits of our society, such as greed and selfishness. But there is also a battle within ourselves. Our own evil tendencies toward self-indulgence and laziness join forces with the greed and selfishness of our society to war against our good intentions to be faithful followers of Christ.

Lent grows short, but there is still time to examine our lives honestly before God. We cannot overcome the enemy until we know who he is.

FRIDAY OF THE FIFTH WEEK OF LENT (II)

Jeremiah was born a priest and was called by God to be a prophet. He warned the people that because of their sins the city of Jerusalem would be destroyed. Such a dire message did not win him approval. He was arrested, beaten, and put in stocks overnight. People refused to accept him for what he was, an authentic spokesman for God.

Jesus was both priest and prophet. He warned that the temple of Jerusalem would be destroyed. This message did not win approval, but it was only one aspect of his teaching which met with opposition. The leaders deeply resented Jesus because, as they put it, he who was only a man was making himself to be God. We know the subsequent events of Jesus' arrest, his passion, and his death.

One might think that this parallel illustrates how Jesus was like Jeremiah. But the opposite is the case. Even though Jeremiah lived some seven centuries before Jesus, he is the follower. Jesus is not like Jeremiah. Jeremiah is like Jesus.

Jesus' claim to be God's Son is true. In his eternal image we have all been created. When he became human, God's plan for all of us took flesh. In looking at the life of Jesus we see what the life of every faithful person will be.

Jesus is the model for our suffering, but also for our joy. We will follow him in death, but we will also be joined with him in his resurrection.

SATURDAY OF THE FIFTH WEEK OF LENT (I)'

Ezekiel promised the people in exile that a day was coming when Israel and Judah would once again be united to form a new kingdom under a new King David.

We believe that this new kingdom is the one which Jesus proclaimed by his preaching and to which he gave birth by his death on the cross. Jesus is the new David and his reign is the kingdom of God.

If there is one goal for which Jesus intensely labored, it is that all his followers might be united as one family in the kingdom of God. He gives us the gift of his life in baptism as the source of our unity.

The life we receive in baptism and which we nourish through the eucharist is not the life which Jesus restored to Lazarus. This friend of Jesus received back his former life so that his time on this earth was extended. The life which Jesus grants to us is his life which will last beyond death.

This life of Jesus is our bond of unity. It forms us into one body, the mystical body of Christ, the Church. Recognizing that the precious life of Christ is our source of oneness should motivate us to want to remove from our lives the obstacle to unity with each other. Sin is that obstacle. Sin separates and divides us from God and each other. It is directly opposed to the gift of divine life within us.

SATURDAY OF THE FIFTH WEEK OF LENT (II)

The Jews who had come to visit Mary, the sister of Lazarus, witnessed the miracle whereby Jesus raised Lazarus from the dead.

We must be clear about the meaning of this miracle. It is not intended to have us think that the promise of eternal life means that we will return from death to the same kind of life which we now enjoy, even though that is what happened to Lazarus. He was raised from the dead so that his time on this earth was extended. The life promised us by God leads us into eternity.

This miracle, like the other signs which Jesus worked, helped receptive people to move toward faith. Eventually they came to recognize that Jesus was proclaiming by words and actions that he is the Son of God. As the unique Son of God Jesus has received the fullness of God the Father's life. If anyone wants a share in this life of God, he must derive it from Jesus who, so to speak, has it all.

As we listen to the gospel and observe the words and actions of Jesus, we receive the grace to deepen our faith in Jesus as God's Son, the source, not of a long life on this earth, but of eternal life in heaven.

Some of Jesus' contemporaries rejected his claim. Others accepted it and became his disciples. By the grace of God we are among those who have embraced Jesus as our Savior and the source of eternal life.

MONDAY OF HOLY WEEK (I)

On this day the death of Jesus was foreshadowed. Six days before passover Mary anointed him in preparation for his burial. This episode near the end of the life of Jesus recalls its beginning when the Magi came to Bethlehem.

The Magi presented Jesus with gifts, the meaning of which were fulfilled during Holy Week: gold symbolized that he is a king; frankincense, that he is a priest; and myrrh, that he is a sacrificial victim.

On Palm Sunday the people hailed Jesus as their King, the meaning of the gold. On Friday Jesus offered himself on the cross as our great High Priest, the meaning of the frankincense. After his death as the victim of sacrifice, the women perfumed his body in preparation for its burial, the meaning of the myrrh.

But there is more. Very early on Sunday morning Mary Magdalene and some other women brought perfumed oils to the tomb to anoint Jesus again. It was almost as if the episode of today's gospel were going to be repeated, except that now Jesus was dead. Or was he? Upon entering the tomb, the women found it to be empty. Jesus as a priest had offered himself as a sacrificial victim, and the Father had exalted him as King by raising him from the dead.

Through the power which God has put into our liturgy we have the privilege this week of living again these events of our salvation.

MONDAY OF HOLY WEEK (II)

On the fourteenth day of the month of Nisan, the day of Passover, the paschal lamb was slaughtered during the evening twilight (Exodus 12). Six days earlier the lamb was selected and prepared. It was on this day that Jesus was anointed in preparation for his burial which would follow his sacrifice as the Lamb of God.

Now on this day, or near it, the diocesan bishop blesses the holy oils. The oil of catechumens is used at baptism and the ordination of priests, the oil of the sick, in the anointing of the sick, and the oil of chrism, in confirmation and the ordination of bishops.

As Christ's body was anointed at Bethany, so the members of his body, his people, are anointed in the sacraments. Blessing the oils at this time shows that the power of the sacraments comes from the Christian paschal mystery, the death and resurrection of Jesus.

More profoundly, this blessing is meant to remind us that each of the sacraments in its own way is a sharing in the one great manifestation of God's love which we call the paschal mystery.

The eucharist is the center and heart of the sacraments, and the other six either lead to it or flow from it. The reason is that the eucharist is the sacrament of the death and resurrection of Jesus, the great event which we are about to commemorate as the climax of our season of Lent.

TUESDAY OF HOLY WEEK (I)

Holy Week bears witness to the great love of Jesus. He is the fulfillment of the suffering servant of the first reading. He is a light to the nations so that salvation may reach to the ends of the earth.

Surely this salvation is for good people only. The abortionists, the drug traffickers, the child molesters are excluded. It is tempting to think that way because we tend to look upon the love of Jesus in human terms. In our experience we respond to those who love us, and we turn aside from those who hurt us.

An important realization emerges from remembering that Jesus' love came to fruition in a garden of betrayal and denial. We understand how Jesus loved his parents. We sense his tenderness with the little children. We appreciate his devotion to his friends, Mary, Martha, and Lazarus. But only divine love could have moved him to die for one who denied him and another who betrayed him.

The early Church was so impressed by this reality of Jesus' love that the New Testament never presents the institution of the eucharist without a mention of the betrayal.

During Holy Week we receive the grace to grow in love for Jesus by seeing what he endured for the salvation of all sinners so that salvation might reach to the ends of the earth. This growth should lead us to a love so deep that it will never tolerate betrayal or denial.

TUESDAY OF HOLY WEEK (II)

Two men emerge from the pages of today's gospel who are distinct and yet similar. They are distinct in that one repented and the other did not. They are similar in that both were too sure of themselves.

The first is Judas, whose name has the same root as the word which designated his nation, Judah. (It would be like our having "Christian" as a first name.) Judas felt that he represented what Judaism stood for, and that Jesus was wrong in his approach. Jesus was changing the rules, the law, the nature of what Judas thought was God's revelation of himself. Judas was also quite certain that Jesus was not going to act in the way that he wanted and expected. Jesus was not only a disappointment to Judas' expectations; he was an affront to his piety.

Peter is the second man. He was devoted to Jesus. The problem was that he was also devoted to himself, to his own power and stamina. He had no doubts that he could do anything for Jesus, even to suffer and die with him. He would do it all, he thought, on his own power.

What was lacking in both men? In one word, humility. Judas did not have the humility to admit that Jesus was right and he was wrong. Peter did not have the humility to recognize that Jesus was strong and he was weak.

We know that love is the essence of being a disciple of Christ. But even love must have a foundation to be solid, and that foundation is humility.

WEDNESDAY OF HOLY WEEK (I)

In some places today is known as Spy Wednesday because this was the occasion when Judas, a contemptible traitor among trusting people, betrayed Jesus.

The love of Jesus blossomed within this soil of hatred. His love is like a beautiful, aromatic rose which rises from a bed of ugly, smelly manure.

Despicable though Judas may be, he helps us to appreciate Jesus. He is a foil to Jesus. In pondering what a hateful crime Judas perpetrated, we come to realize how profound and unselfish the love of Jesus really was.

What the ultimate fate of Judas was, we do not know. But he was included in the saving death of Jesus on the cross. It was up to him, perhaps as he struggled for breath in the last instant of his miserable life, to open his heart to the mercy of the Lord.

Suppose Jesus had died only for Mary, his beautiful mother. It would have been relatively easy to die for such a wonderful, lovable person. In that instance we would not have so readily appreciated how great was the sacrificial death of Jesus. The truth is that Jesus opened his arms on the cross to embrace everyone without exception.

The love of Jesus is seen in that he died not only for Mary, but for Judas and for people like him. And he died for us.

WEDNESDAY OF HOLY WEEK (II)

As we listen to the gospel we hear Jesus solemnly announce, "My appointed time draws near." His mind was filled with a flurry of thoughts. Urging him on was his intense desire to celebrate the Passover with his disciples.

As Jesus was about to repeat the centuries-old ritual as the head of his family of apostles, his mind drifted back to his home in Nazareth. He saw himself as a little boy looking up into the eyes of Joseph who, as the head of the family, presided at the Passover supper. Over the years he had been faithful to this celebration of his people.

Now he knew that this night would indeed be different, not only from every other night, but from every other Passover. When this supper was ended and the morrow had come, he would be dead. He would be the Paschal lamb who takes away the sins of the world. In his death the Christian Passover would be fulfilled.

On the night before his death he gave us the eucharist as the living memorial of his death. This sacrament is the celebration of our Passover, our freedom from sin and death. It is our sacrament of remembering.

People of the eucharist never forget Jesus. But the eucharist is more than remembering. It is reliving the death of Jesus with love. Can we ever forget Jesus? Can we do anything but grow in love for him?

HOLY THURSDAY (I)

This day we celebrate the institution of the holy eucharist on the night before Jesus died. Jesus did not wish to conclude his life on earth without first giving us the holy eucharist, the sacrament of his death and resurrection. In fact, during his life the eucharist gradually became his preoccupation.

When did the idea of the eucharist first occur to Jesus? Perhaps when he was a child eating with his parents, the warmth of that human experience fanned a flame in his mind. Something happened to him at the time of Passover when he was twelve and spent three days in the temple. He was moved closer to the realization that he would become the new temple, and that he would be both priest and victim of his sacrifice.

Other circumstances made him think of the eucharist, such as all the meals he took with his disciples. They made him reflect that human hunger is for something greater than food.

By the time of Passover in the year before he died, the concept of the eucharist was clear in the mind of Jesus. He was preaching along the Sea of Galilee. After the multiplication of the loaves and fishes, Jesus for the first time promised the gift of the eucharist. Jesus said: "The bread that I will give is my flesh for the life of the world. He who eats my flesh and drinks my blood has life everlasting and I will raise him up on the last day." Feeding the five thousand led Jesus to think of the eucharist and to make a solemn promise which he fulfilled on this night.

And there was more. Every act of love, every gesture of affection, every sign of unselfishness and generosity, made him think of the eucharist. The reason is that the eucharist is the sacrament of his death, the greatest act of love the world would ever see. Every event in the life of Jesus was caught up in that one moment of his death, a moment which is a reality for us in the eucharistic sacrifice.

At the Last Supper he washed the feet of his disciples. This was not an example of humility. It was an expression of his love as the servant of his people. It was a eucharistic act because it was part of the supreme love which is the cross.

On Holy Thursday night Jesus said to his disciples: "I have greatly desired to eat this Passover supper with you." He longed for it. He yearned for it. This was the night for the institution of the eucharist. The life and death of Jesus were caught up in that moment and made a permanent reality for his disciples in the holy eucharist. He concluded his act with a command, if not a plea, "Do this in memory of me."

A dedicated disciple follows that command. He centers his life on the eucharist. And how dedicated we would be if everything made *us* think of the eucharist: every meal we enjoy, every hunger of the body we endure, every yearning of the heart we feel, every joy, every sorrow, every affection, every sign of love. It is the Mass, the celebration of the eucharist, that matters. We should long for it. It should be our first thought in the morning and our last thought at night. Would that we could say to Jesus in every eucharistic celebration: "We have greatly desired to eat this supper with you in your memory."

HOLY THURSDAY (II)

Tonight we celebrate the institution of the holy eucharist. How different our religion would be without this wonderful gift. Perhaps one of your first thoughts is the realization that there would be a certain emptiness about our churches without the presence of the Blessed Sacrament. More profoundly there would be no Mass, the heart of our worship. We could have a liturgy of the Word, readings from scripture and prayers, but it would hardly be the same.

There would be no first communion days for little children, brilliant in their white clothing and beautiful in their innocence, no joy of reconciliation for the sinner through the sacrament of penance capped by returning to communion after a long absence, no yearning for the spiritual nourishment and strength which the eucharist alone can give. No martyr would ever have died for the eucharist, and no one with intense conviction would ever declare: "It is the Mass that matters."

We would never hear those beautiful words of Jesus: "Take and eat. This is my body given up for you. Take and drink. This is the cup of my blood, shed for you and for all so that sins may be forgiven." The Christian paschal mystery, the death and resurrection of Jesus, would be lost in a cold and lifeless past. We would not fulfill the words of St. Paul: "When you eat this bread and drink this cup, you proclaim the death of the Lord until he comes."

It is important for us to put the Holy Thursday Mass of the Lord's Supper into perspective. This Mass begins the Sacred Triduum of Good Friday, Holy Saturday and Easter Sunday. Sometimes people wonder why we do not have a Mass on Good Friday, but we do. The Mass of the Lord's Supper is the

Mass of Good Friday. It is like a Mass on Saturday evening which is a Sunday Mass.

If the Mass of Holy Thursday is not understood to be the Mass of Good Friday, the significance of every Mass as the living memorial of the Lord's death and resurrection is obscured. There is much more to the eucharist than the real presence, awesome and sacred though that presence is. Jesus instituted the eucharist as the living memorial of his paschal mystery, the re-presentation of his sacrifice to be perpetuated in the Church until he comes again.

Some Catholics lament the fact that their non-Catholic friends, though devout, do not believe in the real presence of Christ in the Blessed Sacrament. This Mass tonight reminds Catholics that accepting the real presence is not enough. We must remain faithful to the purpose for which Jesus on this night instituted the holy eucharist.

The Second Vatican Council affirmed our tradition in these words: "At the Last Supper our Savior instituted the eucharistic sacrifice of his body and blood to perpetuate the sacrifice of the cross throughout the centuries until he comes again. He entrusted the eucharist to the Church as a memorial of his death and resurrection" (Constitution on the Sacred Liturgy, 47). When we celebrate the eucharist with reverence and love, we enter into the mystery of the death and resurrection of Christ.

GOOD FRIDAY (I)

A long time ago in a galaxy far away a star exploded. Over
uncountable centuries, because of its intense gravity, the star
had been building mass from neighboring celestial bodies.
Then at a time before the creation of the human race, before
there was anyone on this earth who could look up to the
heavens with intelligence and understanding, this immense
star exploded.

On the night of February 23, 1987 an astrologer by the
name of Ian Shelton was working in an observatory in northern
Chile. He looked up to the sky and saw a new star. It was a
supernova. For the first time a human being was seeing the light
of that star which had exploded in the distant galaxy. Ian
Shelton was witnessing an event which had occurred 170,000
years ago. It had taken that much time for the light of the
explosion to reach us.

Less than two thousand years ago in a tiny country on the
other side of the world, an event took place which to all
appearances seemed utterly insignificant, just another Roman
execution of a Jewish upstart. It was all over in a matter of a few
hours, and most of the bystanders were inclined to think no
more of the affair. Without faith they could not even begin to
understand the meaning of what they had witnessed.

We look back upon this event with the eyes of faith. We
believe that on Calvary there was an explosion of God's love. A
new brilliant light had come into the world to show the
meaning and purpose of life. A tremendous power had been
unleashed — the power of God's love.

On the night before he died, Jesus looked up to the
heavens. He saw, not a supernova, but the Passover moon, the

full moon. He knew that it was time for the fullness of God's love. The hour had come for him to pass from this world to the Father. He had loved his own in this world, and would show his love for them to the end, to the very end of his life on the cross. But he wanted this powerful love to touch all of God's people.

And so it was that on Holy Thursday night he gave us the gift of the eucharist, the sacrament of his paschal mystery, the sacrament of his death and his resurrection.

When we celebrate the eucharist, we do not merely look back on something which happened in the past. Although the light of the star which exploded 170,000 years ago is still reaching the earth, the star itself was long ago consumed in a huge thermo-nuclear fire. Not so the death of Jesus. The eucharist brings Jesus' death itself to us, not merely its light. Through the eucharist we are in contact with the saving death of Jesus. The eucharist is his body given up for us, his blood poured out for us. When we eat this bread and drink this cup, we proclaim the death of the Lord until he comes.

I cannot imagine what even an all-wise and all-powerful God could do more to express and communicate his love. If the events of this Holy Week do not move us to deeper faith and greater love, I do not know what will. So that we may never forget but may always grow in our appreciation, Jesus has given us the eucharist, the sacrament of his paschal mystery. The death of Jesus which we commemorate on Good Friday is a reality for us in the celebration of the holy eucharist.

GOOD FRIDAY (II)

Today in the liturgy we hear proclaimed an extraordinary narrative, the story of the passion and death of Jesus Christ. There is a difference between being a witness *of* this event, and a witness *to* this event.

A small number of people were witnesses *of* the death of Jesus: the Roman soldiers, the chief priests, and some of the residents of Jerusalem. They were like people today who see an accident on the highway. Most drive by after only a pause to satisfy curiosity. Some may stop to help the victims. A bold person may even tell the police that he is willing to testify in court because he was, he says, a witness of what happened. But the wisest person does not see any transcendent meaning in the event; if anything, he is frustrated by what appears to be a senseless accident.

At the foot of the cross stood a few people of faith: Mary, the mother of Jesus, some other women, and John. They became witnesses *to* the death of Jesus because through God's grace they began to penetrate its meaning, to see that here was more than an execution, that this death would wipe out sin and death and transform lives. They came to realize this event was a mystery of faith.

The cross stands at the turning point of human history. God's love was poured out upon his creation from the very beginning and was never recalled; his grace was constantly offered to every human person and was never lacking to anyone of good will. And yet because of the death of his Son, God entered into a new covenant with us. This covenant was a pledge of undying love which was sealed in the blood of Jesus Christ.

"For our sake Jesus opened his arms on the cross; he put an end to death and revealed the resurrection. In this he fulfilled the Father's will and won for him a holy people," the people of the new and everlasting covenant (cf. Second Eucharistic Prayer).

We are those people who commemorate the death of Jesus on this Friday which we properly term "Good." God the Father through the gift of faith moves us to go beyond appearances and to see the death of Jesus as more than a tragic execution.

The sacrifice of the cross is so important to us that Jesus has left us the living memorial of his death in the holy eucharist. When we offer the Mass we stand with Mary and the women and John at the foot of the cross.

In our celebration of the eucharist we are called to be witnesses to this death when we proclaim the mystery of faith: "Christ has died, Christ is risen, Christ will come again." We are witnesses to his death when we proclaim: "Dying you destroyed our death; rising you restored our life"; and "Lord, by your cross and resurrection you have set us free; you are the Savior of the world."

This memorial of Good Friday is intended to deepen our appreciation of the cross so that we may enter more fully into the mystery of faith which we celebrate in the holy eucharist.

"The liturgical year, devotedly
fostered and accompanied by the Church,
is not a cold and lifeless representation
of the events of the past,
or a simple and bare record of a former
age; rather, it is Christ himself who is
ever living in his Church."

(*Mediator Dei*, 165)